W9-CCA-532

LEARN TO CROCHET

LEARN
TO
CROCHET

SUE WHITING

NEW
HOLLAND

First published in 2003 by
New Holland Publishers (UK) Ltd
London · Cape Town · Sydney · Auckland

Garfield House, 86–88 Edgware Road
London W2 2EA
United Kingdom
www.newhollandpublishers.com

80 McKenzie Street
Cape Town 8001
South Africa

Level 1, Unit 4, 14 Aquatic Drive
Frenchs Forest, NSW 2086
Australia

218 Lake Road
Northcote, Auckland
New Zealand

Copyright © 2003 text and crochet patterns: Sue Whiting
Copyright © 2003 photographs, illustrations and charts:
New Holland Publishers (UK) Ltd
Copyright © 2003 New Holland Publishers (UK) Ltd

All rights reserved. No part of this publication may be reproduced, stored
in a retrieval system, or transmitted in any form or by any means, elec-
tronic, mechanical, photocopying, recording or otherwise, without the
prior written permission of the publishers and copyright holders.

ISBN 1 84330 386 8

Senior Editor: Clare Sayer
Production: Hazel Kirkman
Design: Frances de Rees
Photographer: Shona Wood
Editorial Direction: Rosemary Wilkinson

1 3 5 7 9 10 8 6 4 2

Reproduction by Pica Digital PTE Ltd, Singapore
Printed and bound by Times Offset (M) Sdn. Bhd., Malaysia

*The publishers would like to thank Baer & Ingram for lending the bedlinen
photographed on pages 54–57. For a mail order brochure, call 01373 813800 or
visit www.baer-ingram.co.uk.*

CONTENTS

	Introduction	6
	Basic Information	8
Technique	The First Stitches	12
Technique	More Stitches	14
Technique	Crochet Diagrams	16
Project	Throw	18
Technique	Working in Rounds	22
Technique	Decreasing Stitches	24
Technique	Joining Seams	25
Technique	Joining in New Yarn and Colours	26
Technique	Increasing Stitches	27
Project	Crochet Bags	28
Project	Dressing Table Set	32
Project	Hats	36
Technique	Stitch Groups	40
Project	Scarves	42
Technique	Working an Edging	46
Technique	Pressing	48
Project	Bedspread	49
Project	Edging	54
Project	Baby Cardigan, Hat and Blanket	58
Technique	Placing the Stitches	66
Project	Baby Blankets	68
Technique	Filet Crochet	72
Project	Filet Curtain Panel	74
	Suppliers	78
	Index	80
	Acknowledgments	80

INTRODUCTION

Crochet is a very relaxing and rewarding craft and is surprisingly easy to do – all you need is a ball of yarn and a crochet hook and you're away!

Once the first few basic stitches are mastered, all the textured and lacy effects are really simple to achieve as they are just combinations of the basic stitches. It's the way the stitches are placed and combined that creates the stunning effects. And once you've learnt how placing of the stitches affects the finished look, everything else is easy.

Crochet is really portable too. You never have more than one stitch on your hook at any time – so there's no risk of "dropping stitches". And, as crochet hooks are much shorter than most knitting needles, your crochet work can easily be tucked into your handbag, ready to pull out whenever you're sitting on a train or waiting for an appointment.

There are very few limits to what you can create in crochet. You can make new "antique" pieces of lace in the classic really fine cotton threads, or stunning textural and multi-coloured jackets and throws using any of the fashion hand knitting yarns available. And remember, you don't have to use crochet to create the whole item. Try livening up a shop-bought or old garment by adding a crochet trim such as a border or a textured motif.

Once you've mastered the basics, let your imagination run riot and you'll soon be creating your own unique crochet masterpieces!

Sue Whiting

Basic Information

Crochet is surprisingly simple and does not require a lot of specialist equipment – all you need is a ball of yarn and a crochet hook and you're ready to go! Once you have assembled your materials there are some basic terms you will need to understand before you begin.

Crochet hooks

Crochet hooks come in a variety of sizes and, nowadays, these sizes are measured on the metric scale although you will often find the old imperial sizes given as well. The smallest crochet hooks are generally made of steel and are used for very fine lace work using yarns not much thicker than sewing thread. Thicker hooks are made of aluminium, and the really big chunky ones, used mainly for very thick yarns, are often made of plastic. Some of the aluminium ones have plastic handles – this makes them more comfortable to hold.

In this book, metric sizes are given for all crochet hooks – use this chart to find the equivalent imperial (old UK) or American size.

Metric	Old UK	USA
0.60 mm	6	-
0.75 mm	5	-
1.00 mm	4	-
1.25 mm	3	-
1.50 mm	2½	-
1.75 mm	2 or 15	5 steel
2.00 mm	14	B/1
2.25 mm	13	-
2.50 mm	12	C/2
3.00 mm	11	-
3.25 mm	10	D/3
3.50 mm	9	E/4
3.75 mm	-	F/5
4.00 mm	8	G/6
4.50 mm	7	7
5.00 mm	6	H/8
5.50 mm	5	I/9
6.00 mm	4	J/10
6.50 mm	3	K/10½
7.00 mm	2	-
8.00 mm	0	-
9.00 mm	00	-
10.00 mm	000	-

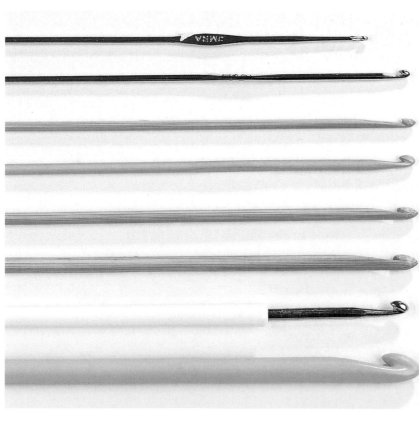

Yarns for crochet

You can use almost any yarn for crochet. There are specialist crochet yarns available but these tend to be very fine cottons and are generally used for delicate lace work using the equally fine steel crochet hooks. Any handknitting yarn is ideal for crochet – simply match the hook size to the thickness of the yarn. As a rough guide, when you are crocheting with a handknitting yarn, use the same size crochet hook as you would have chosen for the knitting needles.

Whilst you can crochet with almost any handknitting yarn, there are certain types of yarn that will be slightly more difficult to use. Obviously a bouclé yarn will not be as easy to loop through and a yarn that is loosely twisted can cause you to split the threads as you work. If you are in any doubt as to whether a yarn will work for crochet, try a swatch before you begin or talk to someone in your local yarn shop.

Other equipment

Apart from the obvious pattern, hook and yarn, you will need a few other items in order to make something in crochet.

A tape measure is important for measuring both the tension of the work and the size of the pieces. Lay the work flat to measure it and avoid the temptation to gently stretch it to the size you want!

For darning in ends and sewing seams, you will need a blunt pointed needle with an eye large enough to thread with the crochet yarn – tapestry needles and needles designed for sewing up hand knits are ideal.

You will also need a pair of scissors to cut the yarn – small embroidery scissors are a good choice. And, if you need to pin pieces together for any reason, use long bead-headed pins as these will hold the pieces better and will not become lost in the work as easily as ordinary dressmaking pins.

Details of anything else you may need to complete the crochet item – such as buttons, elastic or ribbon – should be given with the pattern.

Pressing

Once your crochet work is completed you may need to give it a press. Check the pressing instructions given on the ball band of your yarn and adjust the heat of your iron accordingly. As a general rule, you should avoid pressing on the right side and cover your work with a clean cloth.

Tension

The size of your finished crochet item will be determined by the size of each crochet stitch – and the term used to describe this is the "tension". Each crochet pattern will give details of the tension you need to achieve to ensure your item is the required size and, where there are pieces that need to be joined together, that everything will fit together

BELOW: Apart from your crochet hook and yarn, you will need a few basic items: pins, scissors, needles and a tape measure.

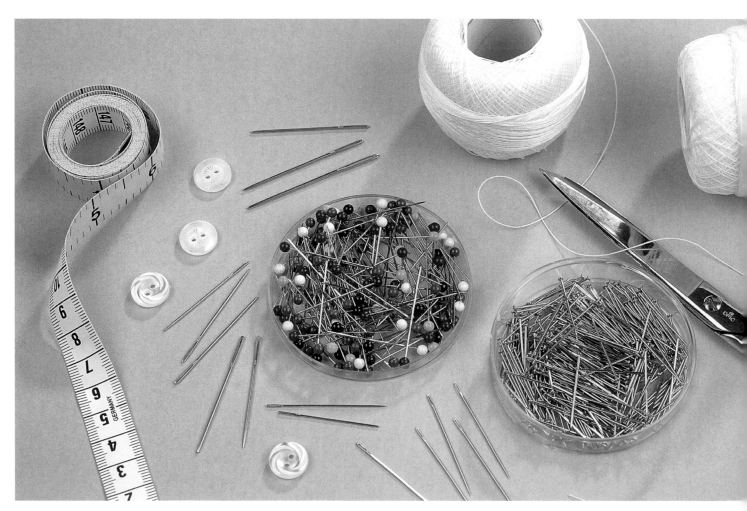

correctly. It is vitally important that you work to this tension – if you do not, the item will not hold its shape properly and you may run out of yarn. The tension is generally given as a number of stitches and rows that need to be achieved within a certain measurement – usually 10 cm (4 in). Sometimes the tension will give the required size of one motif, or the first few rounds of something circular.

Before you begin to make the item, take time to check your tension by working a tension swatch. If the tension is given over 10 cm (4 in), crochet a 13 cm (5 in) square using the stitch pattern for that design. Once the swatch is completed, mark out 10 cm (4 in) in both directions and count the number of stitches and rows you have achieved. If you have more stitches and rows than given in the tension paragraph, you are working too tightly. This means that your item will be too small and the fabric may be too stiff. Try again using a larger size hook. If you have too few stitches and rows, your work is too loose, the item will be too big, you may run out of yarn and the item will be floppy and not hold its shape. Again, work another swatch but this time using a size smaller hook. Continue making swatches until you match the tension of the pattern exactly.

Make a note of the size hook you needed to achieve the correct tension and work the design on that size of hook. Where a pattern uses several sizes of hook, you will need to adjust all these hooks in the same way. If you achieve the tension on a hook one size smaller, use one size smaller hook than stated throughout the pattern.

Sizes

Most of the projects in this book are in just one size. Where designs are in more than one size, the pattern is written for the smallest size with the variations needed for the larger size(s) in square brackets [ ]. Where there is only one set of figures given, this applies to all sizes.

Work the figures in round brackets ( ) the number of times stated after the second bracket.

Abbreviations

Crochet patterns are not written out in full – it would simply take up too much space – but are written in a sort of shorthand, where each crochet term is abbreviated. Use this list of standard crochet abbreviations for all the projects in this book.

beg	beginning
ch	chain
cont	continue
dc	double crochet
dec	decreas(e)(ing)
dtr	double treble
foll	following
htr	half treble
inc	increas(e)(ing)
MS	main shade
patt	pattern
rep	repeat
RS	right side
sp(s)	space(s)
ss	slip stitch
st(s)	stitch(es)
tr	treble
WS	wrong side
yoh	yarn over hook

Sometimes, where a design uses a special stitch or group of stitches, you will find an abbreviation for this term given with the pattern.

Yarn quantities

The quantities of yarn you will need to make the item will be given with the pattern but this is usually based on average requirements. If you decide to make the item slightly bigger or smaller, you will need extra or less yarn. And, if your tension is wrong, you may have a lot of yarn left over or you may run out. As the colour of a yarn can vary very slightly between dye batches, it is advisable to buy all the yarn needed to complete the project at the same time, ensuring all the balls carry the same dye lot number.

The First Stitches

Once you have chosen your yarn and selected your crochet hook you are ready to start. These are the most common and frequently used stitches in crochet.

THE SLIP LOOP

All crochet needs to start with a slip loop. Unlike knitting, there is only ever one stitch on the hook at any time and the slip loop is the starting point for all the stitches that go to make up the finished work.

1. When you make the slip loop, ensure the cut end of yarn is the end you need to pull to tighten the loop. Slip this loop over the crochet hook and pull up the end so the loop sits comfortably around the crochet hook, just below the actual hook section (**A**). The resulting loop on your hook is your first stitch.

A

STARTING TO CROCHET

There are many different ways to hold the crochet hook and the yarn – but the right way is the way you find most comfortable and easiest!

1. Hold the hook in your right hand and the work in your left hand, holding it between the thumb and first finger just below the working stitch (**B**). Traditionally the yarn is held in the

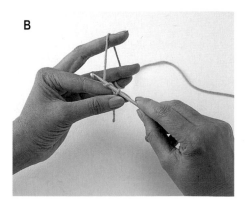

B

left hand but, if you are a knitter, you may find it easier to control if you hold it in your right hand. Whichever hand you hold the yarn in, remember to hold it at an even tension so that each stitch is of the same size.

CHAIN

Almost all crochet will begin with a long chain of simple stitches that are used as the foundation for the rest of the work. These stitches are called "chain" stitches (**abbreviated to "ch"**) and the starting string is called the "foundation chain".

1. To make a chain stitch, wrap the yarn around the hook, bringing it up from the back, over the hook and taking it back to the back below the hook (**C**). Now gently pull this loop of yarn through the loop already on the hook to make the first chain stitch. Remember to use the yarn end that runs to the ball for the stitches – or you will very quickly run out of yarn!

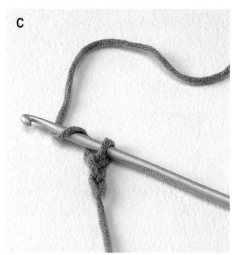

C

2. Continue wrapping the yarn over the hook (**this is abbreviated to "yoh"**) and drawing new stitches through until you have the required number of chain stitches. It is quite easy to count the stitches – along the chain

there will be one neat "V" for each chain stitch (**D**).

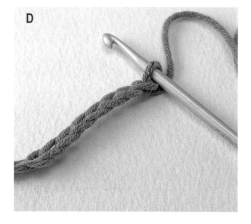

D

Once the foundation chain is complete, you can begin the "real" work!

TREBLE

A treble stitch is one of the most common and frequently used crochet stitches, both for simple and complicated stitch patterns.

1. To make a treble stitch, start by wrapping the yarn around the hook in the same way as for making a chain. Insert the hook into the work – the pattern will tell you exactly where this should be – and wrap the yarn over the hook again (**E**).

E

2. Draw through the new loop. Wrap the yarn around the hook again and draw this loop through the last two loops, leaving just two loops on the hook – the new loop and the original loop (**F**).

F

3. Wrap the yarn over the hook again and pull this loop through the two remaining loops on the hook. The new treble stitch (**abbreviated to "tr"**) is now completed (**G**).

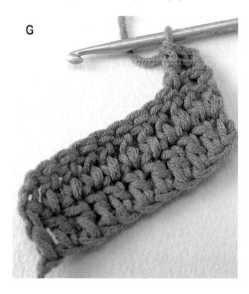

G

POSITIONING THE STITCHES

One of the most important points to remember when following a crochet pattern is to work the new stitches into the correct place. The pattern will tell you exactly where this should be – into a stitch of a previous row or round, into a chain space or into a particular point within the work.

1. Unless a pattern specifies otherwise, when working a new stitch into a previous stitch, insert the hook from the front under both the loops of the "V" of the chain at the top of the stitch (**H**).

H

The only variation to this rule is when working into a chain. Each chain stitch consists of the two bars of yarn that form the "V" and a third bar that sits under these. Work into a chain stitch by insert the hook into the centre of the "V" and under the third bar.

WORKING IN ROWS

Once you have mastered the first few stitches, you are ready to start to put them together to form a crochet fabric. The simplest way to do this is to work them in rows, with the stitches of each row sitting on top of those of the previous row.

Whilst you are working crochet stitches, the hook – and therefore the working loop – are always at the top of the stitch, and crochet stitches are of varying height. It is therefore necessary, at the beginning of a new row of crochet, to work a few chain to bring the hook up to the point it needs to be. These chain are know as the "turning chain" and are usually placed at the beginning of the instructions for the row. Throughout this book, the pattern will tell you what these turning chain stitches are equal to – 3 ch to replace 1 tr, 1 ch to replace a double crochet, 2 ch to replace a half treble, and so on.

1. Once the turning chain have been worked, the actual stitches of the row can be started. Remember that the turning chain sits on the last stitch of the previous row, directly below the first stitch of the new row. So, where you have worked a turning chain of 3 ch (to count as the first treble of the new row), the next stitch you work will be the second stitch of the row. Count away from the hook until you come to the "V" at the top of the next stitch – the first 3 "V"s are the turning chain, the next "V" is the last stitch of the previous row. The new stitch must, therefore, be worked into the next stitch to avoid accidentally increasing or decreasing stitches (**I**).

I

2. At the end of a row, remember to work the last stitch of the row into the top of the turning chain at the beginning of the previous row – or, once again, you risk accidentally increasing or decreasing stitches (**J**).

J

More Stitches

Crochet consists of surprisingly few stitches – it is the way they are put together that creates the varied patterns. The basic crochet stitches vary in height, from the smallest slip stitch to triple trebles, quadruple trebles, and so on.

SLIP STITCH

This is the smallest of all stitches, as it adds no height to the work, and is usually used to join two pieces or to move the hook to a new starting point.

1. To make a slip stitch (**abbreviated to "ss"**), insert the hook into the specified place. Wrap the yarn over the hook in the usual way and draw this loop through both the stitch the hook was inserted through and the working loop (**A**). This completes the slip stitch.

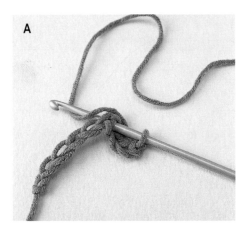

DOUBLE CROCHET

This is a slightly taller stitch, standing about one third the height of a treble. Frequently used for edgings, this is one of the most well known crochet stitches.

1. To make a double crochet (**abbreviated to "dc"**), insert the hook into the required point. Wrap the yarn over the hook and draw a loop through – there are now two loops on the hook.
2. Wrap the yarn around the hook again (**B**) and draw this new loop through both loops on the hook to complete the double crochet.
    When working in double crochet, you will generally find that one chain is added at the

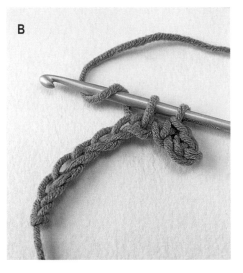

beginning of rows, or rounds, as the turning chain. However, sometimes this does NOT count as the first stitch of the new row, or round, but is simply there to raise the hook to the correct point. Make sure you read the pattern correctly to know exactly where the first stitch should be worked.

HALF TREBLE

This stitch, as its name implies, is basically half a treble stitch and it stands just over half the height of a treble.

1. To make a half treble (**abbreviated to "htr"**), start by making the first half of a treble – wrap the yarn over the hook and insert it into the work as detailed in the pattern. Wrap the yarn over the hook again and draw a loop through – so far, this is as for a treble.
2. There are now three loops on the hook. Wrap the yarn over the hook again and draw this new loop through all three loops on the hook to complete the half treble (**C**).
    A turning chain of two chain is sufficient to replace a half treble.

DOUBLE TREBLE

This stitch is taller than a treble – but it is not, as its name suggests, twice the height. The "double" of its name relates to the number of times the yarn is wrapped around the hook before being inserted into the work.

1. For a double treble (**abbreviated to "dtr"**), wrap the yarn around the hook twice before inserting it into the work (**D**) – for a treble, you would only have wrapped it round once.

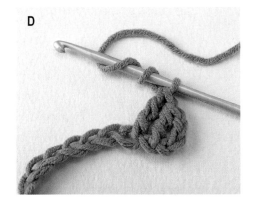

2. Wrap the yarn around the hook again and draw a loop through the work – there are now four loops on the hook. Wrap the yarn around the hook once more and draw this new loop through just the first two loops on the hook, leaving three loops on the hook (**E**).

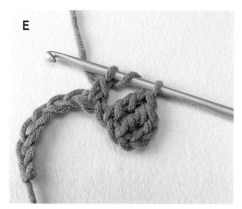

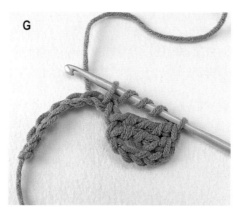

3. Again, wrap the yarn over the hook and draw this new loop through just the first two loops on the hook, leaving two loops on the hook. Wrap the yarn over the hook once more (**F**) and draw this loop through the remaining two loops on the hook to complete the double treble.

You will normally find a turning chain of four chain used to replace a double treble.

2. Now wrap the yarn over the hook and draw this loop through just the first two loops on the hook, leaving four loops on the hook. Repeat this process of wrapping the draw over the hook and drawing the new loop through just the first two loops on the hook until there is just the one, new loop remaining on the hook (**H**).The turning chain used to replace a triple treble is usually five chain.

as many times as necessary to leave just one loop on the hook.

For a quadruple treble (**abbreviated to "qtr" or "quad tr"**) wrap the yarn round the hook four times. For a quintuple treble (**abbreviated to "qtr" or "quin tr"**) the yarn is wrapped around the hook five times. Note that the abbreviation used for both the quadruple and the quintuple treble is often given as "qtr" – this often happens where only one of these two bigger stitches appears in a pattern. Take care to check the abbreviations with a pattern to ensure you are working a stitch of the correct height.

When the yarn is wrapped around the hook six times it creates a sextuple treble (**abbreviated to "str" or "sext tr"**). It is quite easy to continue in this way making bigger and bigger stitches – but they are not often used.

The turning chain needed for these tall stitches is dependant on how many times the yarn is wrapped around the hook. Use this guide below as to how many turning chain are needed for the various stitches.

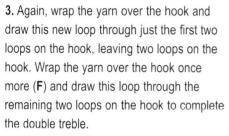

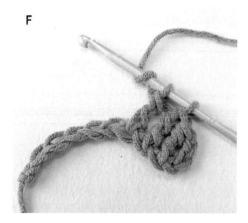

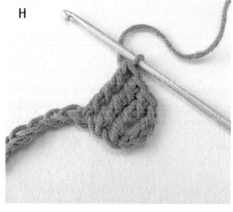

TRIPLE TREBLE

This stitch is taller yet again than those already mentioned and, in the same way that a double treble has a double wrap of yarn round the hook before being inserted into the work, a triple treble has a triple wrapping.

1. Start to make a triple treble (**abbreviated to "ttr"**) by wrapping the yarn around the hook three times. Insert the hook into the work, wrap the yarn over the hook again and draw this new loop through the work. This forms five loops on the hook (**G**).

QUADRUPLE TREBLES AND BIGGER

It is easy to create taller stitches in the same way as for the double and triple treble by increasing the number of times the yarn is wrapped around the hook before it is inserted into the work. No matter however many times the yarn is wrapped around the hook, the way the stitch is worked will not vary. The yarn is wrapped around the hook the number of times needed for this height of stitch. The hook is then inserted into the work, the yarn wrapped around the hook again and then this new loop drawn through. The process of "yoh, draw through 2 loops" is then repeated

STITCH	ABBREVIATION	TURNING CHAIN
double crochet	dc	1 ch
half treble	htr	2 ch
treble	tr	3 ch
double treble	dtr	4 ch
triple treble	ttr	5 ch
quadruple treble	qtr or quad tr	6 ch
quintuple treble	qtr or quin tr	7 ch
sextuple treble	str or sext tr	8 ch

FASTENING OFF

When any piece of crochet is complete, you will need to fasten off the work. When the last stitch has been made, cut the yarn leaving a short end of about 5 cm (2 in). Wrap this end over the hook and draw this loop through the last stitch, continuing to pull the loop until the cut end comes through as well. You can then very gently pull on this yarn end to tighten the last stitch.

Crochet Diagrams

Crochet is a very visual craft, and the key to its success is the correct placement of each stitch in relation to the rest. And, as a visual craft, it is often easiest to see exactly what you are supposed to do by looking at a visual reference – or crochet diagram – that clearly shows where each stitch sits in relation to the others.

Whilst written crochet patterns are easy to follow for simple textured designs, they can become rather long and involved where the design is more complex – such as for a lacy design. In these cases it is often much easier to work the design following a crochet stitch diagram.

These diagrams are basically flat plans of exactly what stitches are worked, in what order and where they are placed in relation to the other stitches and rows. On the diagram, a different symbol is used to replace each type of stitch and the completed diagram will look very similar to the finished work as each symbol will reflect the size of the finished stitch – a tall symbol will be used for a tall stitch and a short symbol for a short stitch.

Accompanying each stitch diagram there should be a key, detailing what each symbol on the chart means. There are standard symbols used for each type of stitch and those used for the basic stitches are listed below:

○	chain
●	slip stitch
✕	double crochet
⊤	half treble
⊤	treble
⊤	double treble
⊤	triple treble
⊤	quadruple treble
⊤	quintuple treble

The base of each symbol will sit over the stitch it is to be worked into. Normally the new stitch will be worked into the top of the stitch below and if this is not the case the symbol for this new stitch will usually be a variation of the symbol for the "standard" version of the stitch. Take time to look at the key that accompanies the chart to make sure you know what each and every symbol means, remembering also to refer to the abbreviations section to understand exactly how to work these stitch variations or groups.

On the stitch diagram, you will also find various symbols to tell you other pieces of information you will need to know – like where to start:

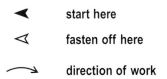

◄	**start here**
◁	**fasten off here**
⟶	**direction of work**

Apart from these symbols, you will also find numbers – these relate to the row or round being worked and usually appear at the beginning of that row or round.

If you choose to follow a stitch diagram, it is best to start by working the foundation chain and the first one or two rows or rounds following the written instructions. This will give you an idea of what shape you are working to. Once this little section is complete, it is usually quite simple to swap over and follow the stitch diagram for each following row or round. But remember to refer back to the written instructions from time to time to make sure you have the correct number of stitches and to know when to do any shaping!

Sometimes a section of the work will be repeated more than once – this is known as the "stitch repeat". On most crochet stitch diagrams the section that needs to be repeated to complete each row or round will generally be indicated – either by a pair of dashed lines or a pair of asterisks. On a circular design, often the whole of the first few rounds will be shown, and after that point only one or two of the stitch repeats will be shown, creating a wedge shaped diagram. Simply follow this "wedge" section, working it repeatedly around the central base section to complete the circle. It is usually quite obvious how many times you need to repeat the wedge – but if you are unsure, it is best to refer to the written instructions for details.

For very simple textured designs with a stitch repeat of one or two stitches – sometimes up to 4 or 5 stitches – the stitch diagram may not tell you how many times you need to work the repeat to fill the row as it should be obvious from the size of the work. Again, if in any doubt, refer back to the written instructions.

Whether you follow the written instructions or the stitch diagram, you should achieve the same results. And often a combination of the two is the easiest option.

A SIMPLE TREBLE FABRIC

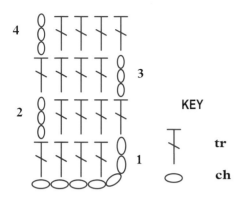

ABOVE: This stitch diagram shows a very simple treble fabric. Here the "stitch repeat" is just one stitch, with one treble being worked into each treble of the previous row, so no stitch repeat is marked on the diagram. It does, however, show how each stitch sits above the stitches of the previous row and how the turning chains are worked and used at each end of the rows.

A TWO-STITCH REPEAT

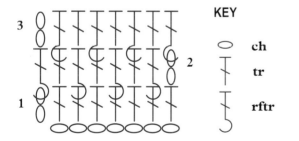

ABOVE: This stitch diagram, as used for the blankets on page 68, is another very simple textured stitch repeat. Here there is just a two stitch repeat and, again, this is not marked on the diagram as it is not really necessary. The stitches used to create this fabric are relief treble stitches – refer to the diagram and key and you will see that the symbol used for each relief treble is a variation of the symbol used for a "standard" treble – it has a little hook on the bottom showing that the stitch is worked in a different way to other trebles.

A THREE-STITCH REPEAT

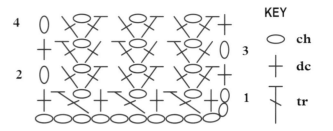

ABOVE: A stitch diagram for a simple three-stitch repeat such as this one, used for the crochet bags on page 28, does not have a stitch repeat marked on it and only shows a total of 11 stitches, even though the actual work is much wider. But what it does clearly show is how to work the beginning and end of every row, and how each group of three new stitches sits above those of the previous row.

A MOTIF STITCH DIAGRAM

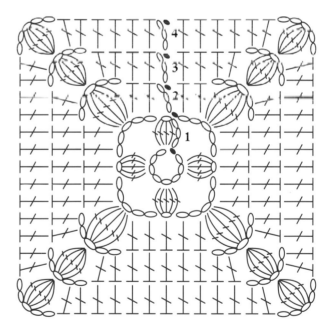

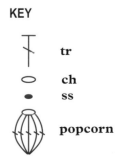

ABOVE: A stitch diagram for a motif such as this one, used for the bedspread on page 49, may just show the first few rounds. By the time these rounds have been completed it should be quite simple to see exactly how each future round is added to complete the full motif.

Throw

Mix natural tones and textures to make this patchwork throw. It's made in strips using the simplest of stitches.

MEASUREMENTS
Finished throw is approx 130 cm (51 in) wide and 150 cm (59 in) long.

MATERIALS
Rowan All Seasons Cotton: 4 x 50 g balls in first colour (A – pale beige)
Rowan Chunky Cotton Chenille: 3 x 100 g balls in second colour (B – beige) and 3 x 100 g balls in fourth colour (D – cream)
Rowan Kid Classic: 4 x 50 g balls in third colour (C – cream)
Rowan Magpie Aran: 2 x 100 g hanks in fifth colour (E – cream marl), and 2 x 100 g hanks in sixth colour (F – cream)
Rowan Rowanspun Aran: 3 x 100 g hanks in seventh colour (G – cream)
5.00 mm (UK 6/USA H8) crochet hook

TENSION
14 sts and 7½ rows to 10 cm (4 in) measured over treble fabric using 5.00 mm hook, or size required to give correct tension.

ABBREVIATIONS
See page 11.

THROW
The throw is worked in 6 striped strips which are sewn together afterwards. When working strips, use 2 strands of Rowan Kid Classic held together and one strand of all other yarns.

First Strip
Using 5.00 mm hook and A, make 34 ch.
Foundation row: 1 tr into 4th ch from hook, 1 tr into each ch to end, turn. 32 sts.
Now work in treble fabric as follows:

Row 1: 3 ch (counts as 1 tr), miss tr at base of 3 ch, 1 tr into each tr to end, working last tr into top of turning ch, turn.
This row forms treble fabric.
Cont straight until Strip measures 20 cm (8 in).
Break off yarn A and join in yarn C.
Cont straight until Strip measures 32 cm (12½ in).
Break off yarn C and join in yarn D.
Cont straight until Strip measures 62 cm (24½ in).
Break off yarn D and join in yarn F.
Cont straight until Strip measures 90 cm (35½ in).
Break off yarn F and join in yarn B.
Cont straight until Strip measures 108 cm (42½ in).
Break off yarn B and join in yarn C.
Cont straight until Strip measures 126 cm (49½ in).
Break off yarn C and join in yarn D.
Cont straight until Strip measures 132 cm (52 in).
Break off yarn D and join in yarn E.
Cont straight until Strip measures 150 cm (59 in).
Fasten off.

Second Strip
Using 5.00 mm hook and G, make 13 ch.
Work foundation row as for First Strip. 11 sts.
Now work in treble fabric as for First Strip as follows:
Cont straight until Strip measures 28 cm (11 in).
Break off yarn G and join in yarn E.
Cont straight until Strip measures 50 cm (19½ in).
Break off yarn E and join in yarn A.
Cont straight until Strip measures 54 cm (21¼ in).

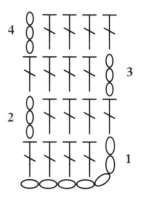

KEY

⊤	tr
⬭	ch

ABOVE: This diagram shows the treble fabric used to make the strips for the throw. At the start of every row, there are 3 turning chain which replace the first treble, and the last treble of every row is worked into the top of the turning chain at the beginning of the previous row. A treble fabric such as this does not really have a stitch repeat as one treble is worked into the top of each treble of the previous row.

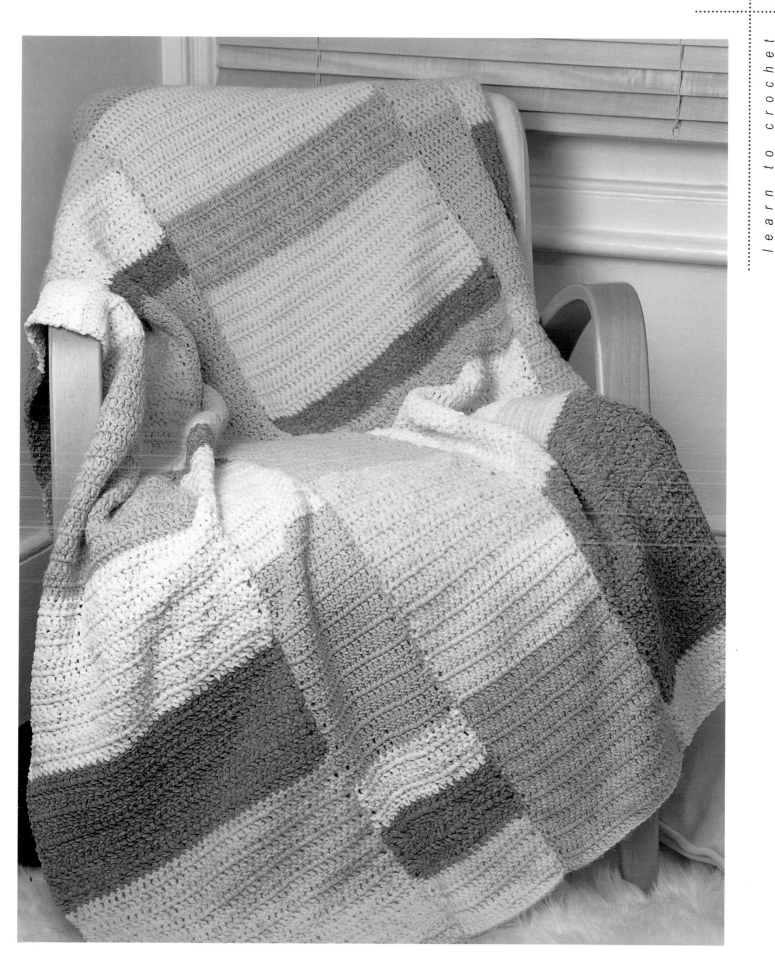

Break off yarn A and join in yarn G.
Cont straight until Strip measures 84 cm
(33 in).
Break off yarn G and join in yarn A.
Cont straight until Strip measures 114 cm
(45 in).
Break off yarn A and join in yarn G.
Cont straight until Strip measures 130 cm
(51 in).
Break off yarn G and join in yarn B.
Cont straight until Strip measures 150 cm
(59 in).
Fasten off.

Third Strip
Using 5.00 mm hook and D, make 51 ch.
Work foundation row as for First Strip.
49 sts.
Now work in treble fabric as for First Strip as
follows:
Cont straight until Strip measures 8 cm
(3 in).
Break off yarn D and join in yarn B.
Cont straight until Strip measures 40 cm
(15¾ in).
Break off yarn B and join in yarn C.
Cont straight until Strip measures 46 cm
(18 in).
Break off yarn C and join in yarn F.
Cont straight until Strip measures 58 cm
(23 in).
Break off yarn F and join in yarn D.
Cont straight until Strip measures 80 cm
(31½ in).
Break off yarn D and join in yarn E.
Cont straight until Strip measures 86 cm
(34 in).
Break off yarn E and join in yarn B.
Cont straight until Strip measures 92 cm
(36¼ in).
Break off yarn B and join in yarn C.
Cont straight until Strip measures 110 cm
(43½ in).
Break off yarn C and join in yarn E.
Cont straight until Strip measures 122 cm
(48 in).
Break off yarn E and join in yarn F.
Cont straight until Strip measures 138 cm
(54½ in).

Break off yarn F and join in yarn A.
Cont straight until Strip measures 150 cm
(59 in).
Fasten off.

Fourth Strip
Using 5.00 mm hook and E, make 30 ch.
Work foundation row as for First Strip.
28 sts.
Now work in treble fabric as for First Strip as
follows:
Cont straight until Strip measures 24 cm
(9½ in).
Break off yarn E and join in yarn F.
Cont straight until Strip measures 34 cm
(13½ in).
Break off yarn F and join in yarn G.
Cont straight until Strip measures 56 cm
(22 in).
Break off yarn G and join in yarn A.
Cont straight until Strip measures 112 cm
(44 in).
Break off yarn A and join in yarn B.
Cont straight until Strip measures 116 cm
(45½ in).
Break off yarn B and join in yarn D.
Cont straight until Strip measures 126 cm
(49½ in).

ABOVE: The seams are clearly visible on the wrong side of the throw – here crocheted seams (see page 25) have been used as they give a neat finish.

Break off yarn D and join in yarn C.
Cont straight until Strip measures 150 cm (59 in). Fasten off.

Fifth Strip

Using 5.00 mm hook and C, make 22 ch.
Work foundation row as for First Strip. 20 sts.
Now work in treble fabric as for First Strip as follows:
Cont until Strip measures 10 cm (4 in).
Break off yarn C and join in yarn B.
Cont straight until Strip measures 16 cm (6¼ in).
Break off yarn B and join in yarn D.
Cont straight until Strip measures 22 cm (8½ in).
Break off yarn D and join in yarn A.
Cont straight until Strip measures 48 cm (19 in).
Break off yarn A and join in yarn F.
Cont straight until Strip measures 64 cm (25 in).
Break off yarn F and join in yarn B.
Cont straight until Strip measures 70 cm (27½ in).
Break off yarn B and join in yarn C.
Cont until Strip measures 84 cm (33 in).

Break off yarn C and join in yarn G.
Cont straight until Strip measures 150 cm (59 in).
Fasten off.

Sixth Strip

Using 5.00 mm hook and G, make 44 ch.
Work foundation row as for First Strip. 42 sts.
Now work in treble fabric as for First Strip as follows:
Cont straight until Strip measures 28 cm (11 in).
Break off yarn G and join in yarn B.
Cont straight until Strip measures 42 cm (16½ in).
Break off yarn B and join in yarn D.
Cont straight until Strip measures 60 cm (23½ in).
Break off yarn D and join in yarn E.
Cont straight until Strip measures 92 cm (36¼ in).
Break off yarn E and join in yarn F.
Cont straight until Strip measures 96 cm (37¾ in).
Break off yarn F and join in yarn D.
Cont straight until Strip measures 108 cm (42¼ in).
Break off yarn D and join in yarn B.
Cont straight until Strip measures 120 cm (47¼ in).
Break off yarn B and join in yarn A.
Cont straight until Strip measures 140 cm (55 in).
Break off yarn A and join in yarn F.
Cont straight until Strip measures 150 cm (59 in). Fasten off.

To Make Up

Matching foundation chain edges, attach the First Strip to the Second, the Second to the Third and so on. Use a large-eyed needle and one of the smooth yarns used in the throw and oversew the edges. If you wish to use crocheted seams, see page 25. Make sure the strips lay smoothly next to each other, without any puckering or pulling. Once all the seams are joined, press carefully from the wrong side, covering the work with a cloth.

Working in Rounds

One of the great joys of crochet is that, as there is only ever one stitch in work, it is very easy to work circular pieces. These circular pieces can either be flat circles, to make a mat or tablecloth, or tubular pieces where no seaming is required afterwards.

Almost all crochet is worked from right to left – so, to create a fabric by working in rows, you need to turn the work at the end of each row before beginning the next row.

When working in rounds, there is no need to keep turning the work. However, as you still need to raise the height of the working loop to the required point for the new round, you will still need to work a "turning" chain at the beginning of each round.

JOINING THE ENDS OF A ROUND

1. When you reach the end of a round, join the end of this round to its beginning by working a slip stitch into the top of the turning chain (**A**). Sometimes, to create a particular effect, you will join the round in a different way – but this will be explained in your pattern.

A

2. Begin the new round by working the required number of turning chain – you will find it called a turning chain whether you turn the work or not! The stitch closing the previous round was worked into the first stitch of the previous row and the turning chain will be standing on this stitch (**B**). So, as when working in rows, the first stitch you work when beginning this new round will be the second stitch of the row.

B

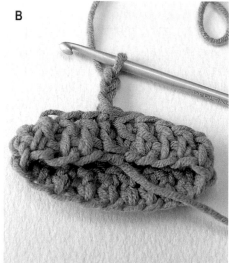

Crochet stitches look different viewed from the front as to when viewed from the back. A crochet fabric made up of rows of trebles will have both sides of the treble stitches showing – one row showing the front of the stitches, with the next row showing their backs.

When making a fabric from trebles where the work is not turned before each new round, only one side of all the trebles will show and the resulting fabric will look very different. To create the same fabric when

working in rounds as to when working in rows, it is essential to turn the work at the end of every round.

Sometimes, to create a particular effect, the pattern will only require you to turn the work at certain points. Make sure you note whether a pattern says to turn the work or not at the ends of the rounds.

STARTING A CIRCULAR PIECE

Working in rounds of crochet can form flat circles of crochet to make mats and tablecloths, or three-dimensional tubes and bowl-shapes to make hats or bags.

Whatever shape you are making you will still, generally, start with a foundation chain.

1. Make the foundation chain as detailed in the pattern and then join the two ends by working a slip stitch into the first chain stitch. Take great care to ensure the chain is not twisted before you join the ends! (**C**)

C

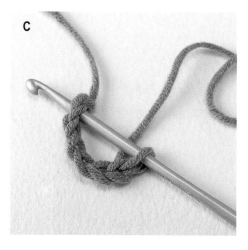

2. Where you have worked a fairly long foundation chain, you will work the first round into the chain stitches in the usual way.

However, if the foundation chain was very short, once the ends are joined you will have a small ring of chain, rather than a large loop. Here the stitches of the first round will often be worked into the centre of this ring (**D**), enclosing the whole of the chain, rather than into each individual stitch. This is often the case when starting a hat at the crown point or a motif or mat at the centre.

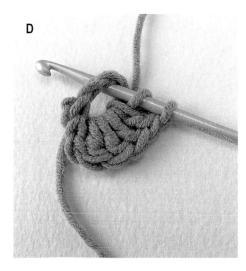

D

You will find that there are normally two to three times as many stitches worked into the ring as there are chain stitches making up the ring – this tends to fill the centre of the ring and, more often than not, there is virtually no hole left at the centre.

CLOSING THE CENTRE HOLE

Sometimes a design will require that there be absolutely no hole left at the centre. In these cases a slip loop is made to replace the foundation chain, and the stitches of the first round are worked into this slip loop.

1. Make a slip loop around the hook but do not tighten it (**E**). Note that this loop is NOT the same as the usual starting slip loop shown on page 12.

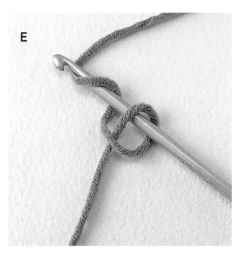

E

2. Now, working into the centre of this loose loop, work the required stitches – when working into a slip loop, these are normally short double crochet stitches (**F**).

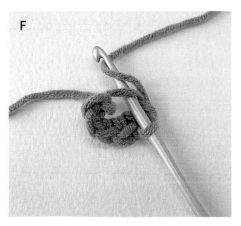

F

3. Once the round is completed, join the ends of the round with a slip stitch. Now gently pull on the loose yarn end to tighten the slip loop and to close the centre hole (**G**).

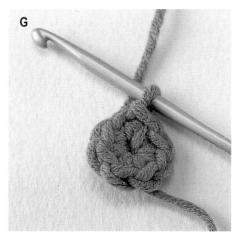

G

FASTENING OFF

When any piece of crochet is complete, you will need to fasten off the work. When the last stitch has been made, cut the yarn leaving a short end of about 5 cm (2 in). Wrap this end over the hook in the normal way and draw this loop through the last stitch, continuing to pull the loop until the cut end comes through as well. You can then very gently pull on this yarn end to tighten the last stitch.

1. When working in rounds, fasten off once the ends of the last round have been joined. Whether working in rows or rounds, if the pieces are to be joined afterwards to make the final item, it is sometimes a good idea to leave a fairly long end when fastening off. This end can then be used to sew any seams, avoiding the need to join in new lengths of yarn and reducing the number of loose ends that need to be darned in (**H**).

H

Decreasing Stitches

When shaping a piece of crochet, there will be times when the number of stitches needs to be reduced. The way this is achieved depends on the amount of stitches to be lost and where these need to be placed along a row or round.

DECREASING AT THE END OF A ROW

1. To reduce several stitches at the end of a row, simply end the row the required number of stitches earlier. For example, to decrease three stitches at the end of the row, work across the row until there are just three stitches left – remember the turning chain at the beginning of the previous row will count as one of these stitches (**A**). Now turn the work and start the next row by working the turning chain. This turning chain will sit on the new row end stitch.

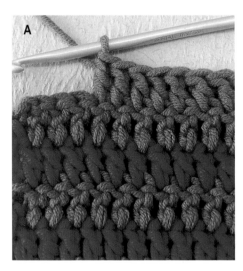

DECREASING AT THE BEGINNING OF A ROW

1. To reduce stitches at the beginning of a row, work slip stitches into each stitch that needs to be decreased and begin the row in the next stitch. For example, to decrease three stitches at the beginning of a row, start this row by working a slip stitch into each of the first three stitches. Now work a slip stitch into the next stitch – the new "first" stitch – and then work the required turning chain before completing the new, shorter row (**B**).

WORKING TWO STITCHES TOGETHER

There are two ways to decrease just one stitch within a row or round. The simplest way is to miss a stitch – but this can leave a hole in the work that can spoil the finished look. The better option is to work two stitches together.

1. To work two treble stitches together, start by making the first treble up to the last "yoh and draw through last 2 loops on hook" point that would complete the stitch. Now work the next treble up to exactly the same point – there are now three loops on the hook (**C**).

2. Wrap the yarn around the hook and draw this loop through, thereby completing both trebles at the same time (**D**).

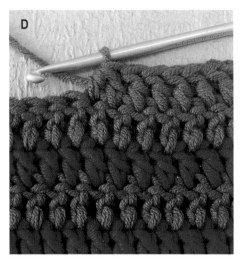

It is possible to decrease in this way when working most stitches – even short, double crochet stitches. Work each stitch up to the last stage and then complete both stitches at the same time.

This method can also be used to decrease more than one stitch – depending on the height of the stitch, up to three or four stitches can be worked together in this way.

This type of decrease has its own abbreviation and this abbreviation will vary depending on the type and number of stitches being used. Working two double crochet together to decrease one stitch will be abbreviated to **"dc2tog"**, whilst working three trebles together to decrease two stitches is abbreviated as **"tr3tog"**.

Joining Seams

Crochet projects are often made up of more than one piece and these separate pieces need to be joined together neatly to create the final item. There are a variety of ways in which pieces can be seamed together.

Because of the nature of crochet fabrics, it will be virtually impossible to create an invisible seam – but the joins can be neat and even. It is best to press the crochet pieces before joining them, and to then press just the seams once they have been sewn.

SEWING SEAMS

Crochet pieces can be joined by hand sewing them together. Use the same yarn for the seams as used to crochet the item and a blunt-pointed needle with an eye large enough to thread with this yarn. Needles designed for sewing up hand knits, or for tapestry, are ideal.

1. Hold the two crochet sections right sides facing and join the seam by over sewing the two edges together, taking in just one strand of yarn along each edge. Place the stitches close together so that the two layers are held together securely. Depending on the amount taken into the seam and the type of crochet stitch, this seam may lie totally flat – or form a slight ridge on the inside (**A**).

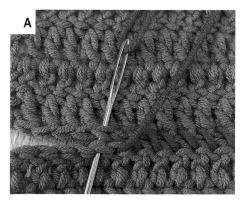

If a perfectly flat seam is required, join the two edges by butting them up against each other. Using the needle and yarn, work a

stitch into one edge and then the other, gently pulling the two edges together as you go along. If worked correctly, the stitching should be invisible and the two edges should sit tightly next to each other. This is not, however, a very flexible seam and is probably best avoided when sewing garment seams.

CROCHETING SEAMS

The most flexible way of joining two pieces of crochet is to work a line of crochet along the edges, working through both edges.

1. Hold the two pieces to be joined right sides facing. Join the two pieces by working a line of double crochet along the edge, inserting the hook through both layers of crochet for each double crochet stitch. Place the stitches quite close to each other and try to take an even amount into the seam – just one strand of yarn from each edge should be sufficient (**B**).

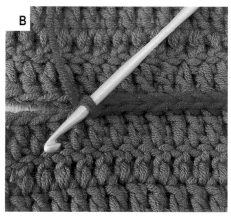

The crochet seam can be worked as a line of slip stitching if preferred. However, whatever stitch is used for the seam, there will be a definite ridge along the seam line on the inside.

JOINING MOTIFS

Depending on the type of motif being made, these either need to be joined together once completed, or they can be joined as the last part of the motif is worked.

1. If the motifs are to be joined as they are made, the pattern will give you details of how this is to be done. Motifs are often held wrong sides together when being joined (**C**).

2. If the motifs are to be joined afterwards, this is best done by crocheting them together. Hold two motifs together and work the crochet along the edges to join them, working one seam stitch for every stitch along the edge of the motif. This seam creates a definite ridge that is sometimes used as a decorative detail – check the pattern to find out whether this seam is to sit on the right or wrong side of the work (**D**).

Joining in New Yarn and Colours

**Most crochet items will use more than one ball of yarn and
many use more than one colour – so you are bound, at
some point, to need to join in a new ball of yarn. This needs
to be done neatly to avoid spoiling the look of the work.**

When working in rows, always try to join in
new balls of yarn at the end of a row – any
long ends left along the side of the work can
be used to join the seams later. If this is not
possible, or when working in the round,
choose a point to join in the new yarn where
you feel it will be both least visible and
easiest to join.

1. To join in new yarn – or a different colour –
at any point, work the last stitch using the old
ball, or colour, up to the point where the last
"yoh and draw this loop through to complete
the stitch" is reached. Now let this yarn fall at
the back of the work and pick up the new
yarn, or colour. Complete the stitch with this
new ball of yarn, leaving two yarn ends at the
back of the work (**A**). Once the crochet is
completed, the yarn ends can be neatly
darned in to the back of the work.

2. Depending on the type of stitch pattern
being worked, it is possible to enclose the
ends of the yarn inside the following stitches.
Simply let them sit on top of the previous row,
between the "V"s of the stitches, and work
the next five or six stitches enclosing these
ends as well (**B**). Leave the ends free at the
back of the work beyond this point and, afterwards, gently pull on the yarn ends and trim
away the excess.

When joining in yarn to work a new section
– such as an edging – join in the new yarn by
first making a slip loop around the hook. Now
work a slip stitch into the crochet work at the
point where the yarn needs to be joined in.
You are then ready to start the row or round.

Increasing Stitches

If you are making a shaped piece of crochet you will not only need to work decreases but you will also need to add extra stitches as well. The way this is done will depend on where the increased stitches need to fall within the work.

Not every crochet section will be just a tube or rectangle – sometimes you will need to shape the work by increasing its width and the number of stitches in each row or round. Depending on the effect to be achieved there are many ways this can be done.

TO INCREASE ONE STITCH AT ANY POINT

1. To increase one stitch at any point within a row, or round, work two stitches into the same point on the previous row or round (**A**).

If you need to increase by more than one stitch, this can be done in the same way – simply work the required number of stitches into the same place. Take care though as too many stitches worked into one place can distort the work. If you need to increase by more than three stitches, it is best to evenly spread out the increased stitches over the whole row or round, working two stitches into one at evenly spaced intervals.

Working several stitches into a particular point is also used to create fancy stitch patterns. Here, lots of stitches are worked

into one base stitch and then the same number of stitches are missed when working on along the row or round, thereby keeping the final number of stitches the same. Before you work any "increases" of this sort, check that the pattern means to increase stitches, rather than just create an effect!

TO INCREASE SEVERAL STITCHES AT THE BEGINNING OF A ROW

1. To increase at the beginning of a row, you will need to make a foundation chain for these new stitches. Before beginning the row, work a chain for each new stitch needed and then work the required turning chain for the type of stitch being used. You can then work the new stitches as needed, continuing on across the previous row (**B**).

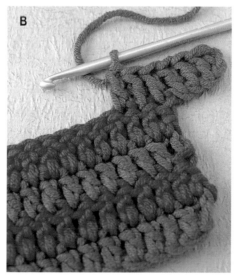

For example, to increase three trebles at the beginning of a row, make three chain (one for each new stitch) and then a further two chain. These last three chain form the first stitch, so the second new (treble) stitch

will be worked into the fourth chain counting away from the hook. The third increased stitch will be worked into the next chain and the following stitch will be worked into the last stitch of the previous row.

TO INCREASE SEVERAL STITCHES AT THE END OF A ROW

1. To increase several stitches at the end of a row, make a new separate foundation chain for these stitches. For example, to increase five stitches at the end of a row, make a foundation chain of five chain using an oddment of the main yarn. Work across the row to the end of the row until the stitch has been worked into the top of the turning chain at the beginning of the previous row. Now work stitches into each of the new foundation chain stitches before turning the work (**C**).

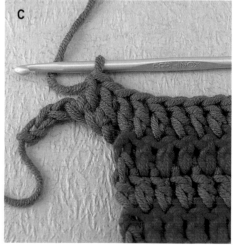

When working a complex stitch pattern, or a lacy design, you will generally find that the row, or round, instructions will be written to include any necessary increases so that the pattern will follow through correctly.

Crochet Bags

You can shop till you drop and not worry about carrying it all home when you make these useful bags.

MEASUREMENTS

Shopper is approx 32 cm (12½ in) wide and 30 cm (12 in) tall.
Cross-body bag is approx 16 cm (6¼ in) wide and 20 cm (7¾ in) tall.

KEY

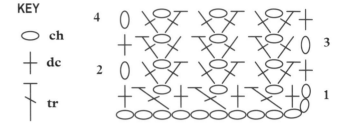

MATERIALS

For the Shopper:
3 x 100 g balls of Wendy Supreme Luxury Cotton DK in Main Colour (M - beige)
1 ball of same yarn in Contrast Colour (C - white)
For the Cross-body bag:
3 x 50 g balls of Rowan Denim
1 button
For either bag:
3.50 mm (UK 9/USA E4) and 3.00 mm (UK 10/USA D3) crochet hooks

TENSION

Shopper: 25 sts and 15 rows measured over the textured pattern, 20 sts and 14 rows measured over the half treble fabric to 10 cm (4 in) using 3.50 mm hook, or size required to give correct tension.
Cross-body bag: Before washing, 21 sts and 13 rows, after washing 25 sts and 15 rows measured over the textured pattern, 20 sts and 14 rows measured over the half treble fabric to 10 cm (4 in) using 3.50 mm hook, or size required to give correct tension.
Note: Rowan Denim yarn shrinks when washed. Allowances have been made in the Cross-body Bag pattern for this shrinkage.

ABBREVIATIONS

htr2tog = (yoh and insert hook as indicated, yoh and draw loop through) twice, yoh and draw through all 5 loops on hook.
See also page 11.

BAGS

SIDES (Make 2)

Using 3.50 mm hook and M, make 81 ch.
Row 1: (1 dc, 1 ch and 1 tr) into 3rd ch from hook, miss 2 ch, *(1 dc, 1 ch and 1 tr) into next ch, miss 2 ch, rep from * to last ch, 1 dc into last ch, turn. 26 patt repeats, 80 sts.
Row 2: 1 ch (counts as first st), miss (1 dc and 1 tr) at end of last row, *(1 dc, 1 ch and 1 tr) into next ch sp**, miss (1 dc and 1 tr), rep from * to end, ending last rep at **, 1 dc into top of turning ch, turn.
Row 2 forms textured patt.
Cont in textured patt until work measures 18 cm (7 in).
Join in C and work 2 rows.
Using M work a further 6 rows.
Using C, work another 2 rows.

ABOVE: This stitch diagram shows the stitch pattern used for the lower section of both bags. Each row of the pattern consists of groups of a double crochet, chain and treble that sit on top of the matching group of the previous row. At the beginning of each row, work one chain to bring the new row up to the required height, and complete the row by working a double crochet into the chain at the beginning of the previous row. Between these two stitches, repeat the groups of 3 stitches as many times as required.

NOTE:
Pattern is written for the Shopper, followed by the Cross-body bag in bold in square brackets. Where only one set of figures is given, this refers to both bags. For Cross-body bag, ignore references to M and C and use same colour throughout.

LEFT: The shopper is the larger of the two bags and has two bold stripes in a contrasting colour.

Break off C and cont using M only.
Cont straight until work measures
27 [**20**] cm (10½ [**7¾**] in).
Change to 3.00 mm hook.
Next row: 2 ch (counts as first st), *1 htr into each of next 2 sts, htr2tog over next 2 sts**, 1 htr into next st, rep from * to end, ending last rep at ** and working last htr into top of turning ch, turn. 64 sts.
Next row: 2 ch (counts as first htr), 1 htr into each htr to end, working last htr into top of turning ch, turn.
Rep last row until work measures 32 [**24**] cm (12½ [**9½**] in).
Fasten off.

Shape first strap
Miss first 6 [**8**] sts of next row, rejoin yarn to next st with a ss and cont as follows:-
**Row 1: 2 ch, miss st at base of 2 ch, 1 htr

Shape second strap
Return to last complete row worked, miss 20 [**16**] sts after first strap, rejoin yarn to next st with a ss and work second strap to match first from ** to **.
Holding straps with RS tog and taking care not to twist straps, join ends of straps by working a row of dc through sts of both straps.
Fasten off.

To Make Up
Shopper only: Join Sides together along side edges and base. Using 3.00 mm hook and M, work one round of dc evenly around edges of straps and upper edge, ending with ss to first dc. Press.
Cross-body bag only: Fold bag in half to form a tube and join row ends to form back

into each of next 15 sts, turn. 16 sts.
Row 2: 2 ch (counts as first st), htr2tog over next 2 sts, 1 htr into each st to last 3 sts, htr2tog over next 2 sts, 1 htr into top of turning ch, turn.
Rep row 2, 5 times more. 4 sts.
Row 8: 2 ch (counts as first st), 1 htr into each st to end, working last htr into top of turning ch, turn.
Rep row 8 only until strap measures
35 [**70**] cm (13¾ [**27½**] ins).
Fasten off.**

seam. Re-fold bag so that seam runs centrally down back between folds and sew base seam. Using 3.00 mm hook, work one round of dc evenly around edges of strap and upper edge, ending with ss to first dc and working button loop midway across front edge of bag as follows: 9 ch, turn, 1 dc into 5th ch from hook, 1 dc into each of next 4 ch. Sew on button to correspond with button loop. Machine wash bag on a hot setting to shrink bag to correct size. Press.

Dressing Table Set

Adorn your dressing table with these little lacy mats. The larger mat is made by simply making seven of the smaller mats and joining them together. Try joining more motifs, honeycomb style, to create a mat or cloth of any size.

MEASUREMENTS
Finished small mat is 11 cm (4¼ in) in diameter. Finished large mat is 27 cm (10½ in) in diameter.

MATERIALS
2 x 10 g balls of Anchor Pearl Cotton no 8 in white
2.00 mm (UK 14/USA B1) crochet hook

TENSION
First 3 rounds measures 4.5 cm (2 in) in diameter using 2.00 mm hook, or size required to give correct tension.

ABBREVIATIONS
tr4tog = *yoh and insert hook as indicated, yoh and draw loop through, yoh and draw through 2 loops, rep from * 3 times more, yoh and draw through all 5 loops on hook.
tr5tog = *yoh and insert hook as indicated, yoh and draw loop through, yoh and draw through 2 loops, rep from * 4 times more, yoh and draw through all 6 loops on hook.
See also page 11.

SMALL MAT

Using 2.00 mm hook, make 6 ch and join with a ss to form a ring.

Round 1: 1 ch, 12 dc into ring, ss to first dc.

Round 2: 1 ch, 1 dc into st at base of 1 ch, [7 ch, miss 1 dc, 1 dc into next dc] 5 times, 3 ch, 1 dtr into top of dc at beg of round.

Round 3: 3 ch, 4 tr into ch sp formed by dtr at end of previous round, [3 ch, 5 tr into next ch sp] 5 times, 3 ch, ss to top of 3 ch at beg of round.

Round 4: 3 ch, miss st at base of 3 ch, 1 tr into each of next 4 tr, *3 ch, 1 dc into next ch sp, 3 ch**, 1 tr into each of next 5 tr, rep from * to end, ending last rep at **, ss to top of 3 ch at beg of round.

Round 5: 3 ch, miss st at base of 3 ch, tr4tog over next 4 tr, *[5 ch, 1 dc into next ch sp] twice**, 5 ch, tr5tog over next 5 tr, rep from * to end, ending last rep at **, 2 ch, 1 tr into top of tr4tog at beg of round.

Round 6: 1 ch, 1 dc into ch sp formed by tr at end of previous round, [5 ch, 1 dc into next ch sp] 17 times, 2 ch, 1 tr into top of dc at beg of round.

Round 7: 1 ch, 1 dc into ch sp formed by tr at end of previous round, *3 ch, (5 tr, 3 ch and 5 tr) into next ch sp, 3 ch, 1 dc into next ch sp, 5 ch**, 1 dc into next ch sp, rep from * to end, ending last rep at **, ss to top of dc at beg of round.
Fasten off.

LARGE MAT

Large mat is 7 of the small mats joined together – one central "mat" with 6 more surrounding it. Each "mat" is a hexagon and these hexagons can be joined after they are made by sewing them together where they meet at the corners and midway along the sides. Alternatively they can be joined whilst the last round is being worked. To join them whilst working round 7, replace the (3 ch) at the corner to be joined with (1 ch, 1 ss into

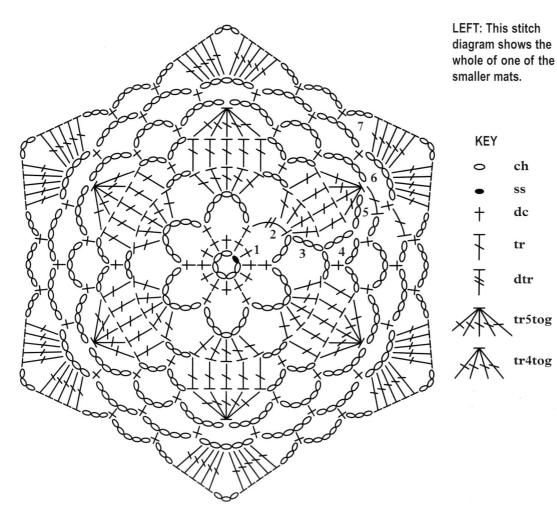

LEFT: This stitch diagram shows the whole of one of the smaller mats.

KEY

o	ch
•	ss
†	dc
⊤	tr
⊤	dtr
⋏	tr5tog
⋀	tr4tog

corresponding ch loop on adjacent hexagon, 1 ch), and replace the (5 ch) at the centre of a side with (2 ch, 1 ss into corresponding ch loop on adjacent hexagon, 2 ch). Join hexagons holding them with WS together.

To Finish

Pin out to measurement given, dampen and leave to dry naturally.

Hats

**These delightful sun hats are great for children
of all ages – choose from bright sunny colours for
a toddler to subtler colours for older children.**

MEASUREMENTS

To fit average size toddler [child:adult] head
Width around head is 44 [49:53] cm (17¼
[19¼:20¾] in).

MATERIALS

For a hat in one colour: 2 [3:3] x 50 g
balls of Rowan Handknit DK Cotton
3.50 mm (UK 9/USA E4) crochet hook
Toddler's hat used 1 ball in each of four
colours – green, orange, yellow and red
Child's hat used 1 ball in each of 3
colours – navy, turquoise and green
Adult's hat used 2 balls in each of 2
colours – dark beige and mid beige

TENSION

18 sts and 12 rows to 10 cm (4 in) measured
over half treble fabric using 3.50 mm hook,
or size required to give correct tension.

ABBREVIATIONS

See page 11.

ONE COLOUR HAT

Using 3.50 mm hook, make 4 ch and join
with a ss to form a ring.
Round 1: 2 ch (counts as 1 htr), 7 htr into
ring, ss to top of 2 ch at beg of round. 8 sts.
Round 2: 2 ch (counts as 1 htr), 1 htr into st
at base of 2 ch, 2 htr into each of next 7 htr,
ss to top of 2 ch at beg of round. 16 sts.
Round 3: 2 ch (counts as 1 htr), 1 htr into st
at base of 2 ch, 1 htr into next htr, (2 htr into
next htr, 1 htr into next htr) 7 times, ss to top
of 2 ch at beg of round. 24 sts.
Round 4: 2 ch (counts as 1 htr), 1 htr into st
at base of 2 ch, 1 htr into each of next 2 htr,

(2 htr into next htr, 1 htr into each of next
2 htr) 7 times, ss to top of 2 ch at beg of
round. 32 sts.
Round 5: 2 ch (counts as 1 htr), 1 htr into st
at base of 2 ch, 1 htr into each of next 3 htr,
(2 htr into next htr, 1 htr into each of next
3 htr) 7 times, ss to top of 2 ch at beg of
round. 40 sts.
Round 6: 2 ch (counts as 1 htr), 1 htr into st
at base of 2 ch, 1 htr into each of next 4 htr,
(2 htr into next htr, 1 htr into each of next
4 htr) 7 times, ss to top of 2 ch at beg of
round. 48 sts.
Round 7: 2 ch (counts as 1 htr), 1 htr into st
at base of 2 ch, 1 htr into each of next 5 htr,
(2 htr into next htr, 1 htr into each of next
5 htr) 7 times, ss to top of 2 ch at beg of
round. 56 sts.
Round 8: 2 ch (counts as 1 htr), 1 htr into st
at base of 2 ch, 1 htr into each of next 6 htr,
(2 htr into next htr, 1 htr into each of next
6 htr) 7 times, ss to top of 2 ch at beg of
round. 64 sts.
Round 9: 2 ch (counts as 1 htr), 1 htr into st
at base of 2 ch, 1 htr into each of next 7 htr,
(2 htr into next htr, 1 htr into each of next
7 htr) 7 times, ss to top of 2 ch at beg of
round. 72 sts.
Round 10: 2 ch (counts as 1 htr), 1 htr into
st at base of 2 ch, 1 htr into each of next
8 htr, (2 htr into next htr, 1 htr into each of
next 8 htr) 7 times, ss to top of 2 ch at beg of
round. 80 sts.

Child and adult sizes only

Round 11: 2 ch (counts as 1 htr), 1 htr into
st at base of 2 ch, 1 htr into each of next
9 htr, (2 htr into next htr, 1 htr into each of
next 9 htr) 7 times, ss to top of 2 ch at beg of
round. 88 sts.

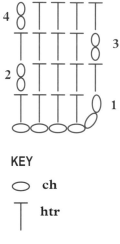

KEY

⬯ ch

⊤ htr

ABOVE: This stitch
diagram shows the
basic half treble fabric
used for the hats.
Although this diagram
shows the fabric as
rows, the turning
chains shown here at
the beginning of each
row will still be worked
for each new round. At
the end of every round,
work a slip stitch into
the top of this turning
chain to close the
round. The turning
chain for the new
round will sit on top of
the turning chain of
each previous row.

Adult size only

Round 12: 2 ch (counts as 1 htr), 1 htr into st at base of 2 ch, 1 htr into each of next 10 htr, (2 htr into next htr, 1 htr into each of next 10 htr) 7 times, ss to top of 2 ch at beg of round. 96 sts.

All sizes

Next round: 2 ch (counts as 1 htr), 1 htr into each htr to end, ss to top of 2 ch at beg of round.
Rep last round 7 [8:9] times more.
Shape brim
Round 1: 2 ch (counts as 1 htr), 1 htr into st at base of 2 ch, 1 htr into each of next 7 htr, *2 htr into next htr, 1 htr into each of next 7 htr, rep from * to end, ss to top of 2 ch at beg of round. 90 [99:108] sts.

Round 2: 2 ch (counts as 1 htr), 1 htr into each htr to end, ss to top of 2 ch at beg of round.

Round 3: 2 ch (counts as 1 htr), 1 htr into st at base of 2 ch, 1 htr into each of next 8 htr, *2 htr into next htr, 1 htr into each of next 8 htr, rep from * to end, ss to top of 2 ch at beg of round. 100 [110:120] sts.

Round 4: 2 ch (counts as 1 htr), 1 htr into each htr to end, ss to top of 2 ch at beg of round.

Round 5: 2 ch (counts as 1 htr), 1 htr into st at base of 2 ch, 1 htr into each of next 9 htr, *2 htr into next htr, 1 htr into each of next 9 htr, rep from * to end, ss to top of 2 ch at beg of round. 110 [121:132] sts.

Round 6: 2 ch (counts as 1 htr), 1 htr into each htr to end, ss to top of 2 ch at beg of round.

ABOVE: In smart blues and greens, this three-colour hat could be adapted for any age.

ABOVE: This colourful hat is perfect for a toddler.

Child and adult sizes only

Round 7: 2 ch (counts as 1 htr), 1 htr into st at base of 2 ch, 1 htr into each of next 10 htr, *2 htr into next htr, 1 htr into each of next 10 htr, rep from * to end, ss to top of 2 ch at beg of round. [132:144] sts.

Round 8: 2 ch (counts as 1 htr), 1 htr into each htr to end, ss to top of 2 ch at beg of round.

Adult size only

Round 9: 2 ch (counts as 1 htr), 1 htr into st at base of 2 ch, 1 htr into each of next 11 htr, *2 htr into next htr, 1 htr into each of next 11 htr, rep from * to end, ss to top of 2 ch at beg of round. 156 sts.

Round 10: 2 ch (counts as 1 htr), 1 htr into each htr to end, ss to top of 2 ch at beg of round.

All sizes

Now work one round of crab st (dc worked from left to right, instead of right to left) around lower edge of hat.
Fasten off.

FOUR COLOUR HAT

Work as given for one colour hat (but change colour every 2 rounds using all 4 colours in sequence).

THREE COLOUR HAT

Work as given for one colour hat but work 2 rounds in each of the three colours.

TWO COLOUR HAT

Work as given for one colour hat but work 4 rounds in each of the two colours.

Stitch Groups

Most crochet stitch patterns are created by the way the various stitches are combined and by the positions in which these stitches are worked. There are a few well known stitch groups that have their own names – shells, picots, clusters, bobbles, popcorns and puff stitches.

The names given to these stitch groups relate not to the actual stitch used, but to the way the stitches are grouped together. A shell, cluster or popcorn can contain any number of stitches and these stitches can be of any size.

SHELLS

A shell, or fan, is usually made up of several of the same type of stitch worked into the same place to create a shell- or fan-like effect.

Normally all the stitches that go to make up the shell will be worked into just one stitch, rather than into a chain space. This helps to hold the base of the shell together, leaving the upper ends of the stitches to fan out (**A**).

PICOT

A picot is basically a loop of chain stitches that sit on the edge of the crochet to form a little knot or bead.

Picots can be made up of any number of chain stitches – although, most commonly, they will contain either three or four chain. This little loop of chain is then secured by working a stitch into the same place as where the picot began. This can be achieved by working a slip stitch into the first of the picot chain, or by working a double crochet into the stitch the picot chain sits on (**B**). Take care to read the pattern so that you know exactly how the picots are to be worked.

CLUSTER

A cluster is a group of stitches that are joined together at the top. The effect created is similar to that of a shell or fan – but the other way up.

Clusters are usually made up of stitches at least as tall as a treble, and the base of each stitch that forms the cluster is usually worked into a different stitch. The pattern should explain exactly where the hook should be inserted for each of the stitches making up the cluster. To work a cluster, start by working the first stitch of the group up to the point where there are two loops left on the hook. Now work each of the other stitches to exactly the same stage, remembering to insert the hook at the points detailed in the pattern. You will now have one more loop on your hook than there are stitches making up the cluster – a three treble cluster will have four loops on the hook at this point. Take the yarn over the hook again and draw this new loop through all the loops on the hook to close the top of the cluster and complete the stitch group (**C**).

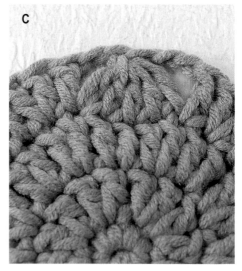

BOBBLES

A crochet bobble will, as its name suggests, create a bobble of yarn on the fabric surface (**D**).

Bobbles are worked in exactly the same way as a cluster except all the stitches that go to make up the bobble will be worked into the same place, thereby pulling together both the top and the bottom of the stitches. To ensure the top of a bobble is closed sometimes a chain stitch will be worked to secure it.

POPCORNS

Popcorns are similar to a shell but the two sides of the group are bought together to form the stitches into a tiny cup (**E**).

To make a popcorn, work the stitches as detailed in the pattern – these will usually be stitches at least at tall as a treble and they will probably all be worked into one stitch. When this first stage is complete, take the hook out of the working loop. Insert the hook back through the top of the first stitch of the popcorn, pick up the working loop again and draw the working loop through the top of the first stitch, thereby bringing together the first and last stitches of the popcorn.

As with a bobble, it is sometimes best to secure the top of a popcorn by working a chain stitch – check the pattern you are following to see if this is needed. If a popcorn is being worked on a wrong side row or round, ensure that the stitches are gently pushed through so that the popcorn stands proud on the right side of the work.

PUFFS

Puffs are similar to bobbles but they generally use half treble stitches. The height of the resulting puff is created by extending the size of the loops that are drawn through the work.

Begin by starting to work a half treble stitch. Take the yarn round the hook and insert the hook as detailed. Take the yarn over the hook again and draw this loop through the work. The height of the puff is determined by the length of this loop drawn through the work. Repeat this process as many times as required – you will end up with two loops for every half treble started plus one extra loop. Now take the yarn over the hook again and draw this new loop through all the loops on the hook to complete the puff. It is sometimes necessary to secure the top of a puff with a chain stitch (**F**).

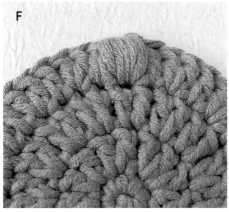

Where a pattern regularly uses a particular stitch group you may find that the instructions will refer to working "1 cluster into next stitch", rather than spelling it out in full every time. Exactly how this cluster should be worked will be explained in the abbreviations accompanying the pattern. Sometimes two different types of the same stitch group will

appear within one design – you could have a shell of four trebles (abbreviated to "4 tr shell") in one place but a shell made up of seven trebles (abbreviated to "7 tr shell") elsewhere. Make sure you read the pattern and the abbreviations before you begin to ensure you work each stitch group correctly.

CRAB STITCH

Almost all crochet is worked from right to left. The exception to this rule is crab stitch. This is simply double crochet worked in the "wrong" direction – from left to right, instead of right to left. As the stitches are worked back on themselves, they create a neat knotted effect that is often used as an edging. It is not possible to see the "V"s that make up the stitches and, therefore, you will very rarely find another line of stitching worked into crab stitch.

Crab stitch can sometimes take a while to get the hang of – mainly because you feel you should be doing something different. It is just double crochet worked from left to right, instead of right to left.

1. Insert the hook into the next stitch from front to back in exactly the way you would normally – but use the stitch to the right, not the left, twisting the hook back on itself.
2. Wrap the yarn around the hook in the normal way and draw this loop through the work (**G**). Take the yarn over the hook again and draw this loop through both loops on the hook to complete the stitch.

Scarves

Combine a lacy stitch with luxury yarn to make these cosy scarves. Choose either the fluffy version for casual wear, or the sophisticated shorter version in silk for a smarter look.

MEASUREMENTS

Long scarf is approx 22 cm (8½ in) wide and 180 cm (71 in) long (excluding fringe)

Short scarf is approx 20 cm (8 in) wide and 115 cm (45¼ in) long

MATERIALS

For the long scarf:

4 x 50 g balls of Rowan Kid Soft in magenta

5.00 mm (UK 6/USA H8) crochet hook

For the short scarf:

3 x 50 g balls of Jaeger Silk 4 ply in purple

2.50 mm (UK 12/USA C2) crochet hook

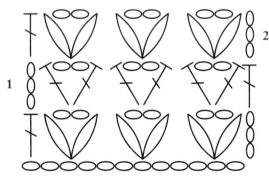

KEY

○ ch

† tr

⬭ cluster

TENSION

Long scarf (above): 4 patt repeats (16 sts) to 11 cm and 12 rows to 12 cm (4½ in) using 5.00 mm hook, or size required to give correct tension.

Short scarf (below): 9 patt repeats (36 sts) to 13 cm (5 in) and 16 rows to 15 cm (6 in) using 2.50 mm hook, or size required to give correct tension.

ABBREVIATIONS

cluster = *yoh and insert hook as indicated, yoh and draw loop through lengthening loop to approx 10mm for long scarf or 7mm for short scarf, yoh and draw through 2 loops on hook, rep from * once more, yoh and draw through 2 loops on hook, yoh and draw through last 2 loops on hook.
See also page 11.

ABOVE: This stitch diagram shows the stitches used for both scarves.

LONG SCARF

Using 5.00 mm hook, make 35 ch.

Foundation row: Miss 4 ch (counts as 1 tr and 1 ch), *(1 cluster, 2 ch and 1 cluster) into next ch, miss 3 ch, rep from * to last 3 ch, (1 cluster, 2 ch and 1 cluster) into next ch, miss 1 ch, 1 tr into last ch, turn. 8 patt repeats, 34 sts.

Now work in patt as follows:

Row 1: 3 ch (counts as 1 tr), (1 tr, 2 ch and 1 tr) into each ch sp to end, 1 tr into top of turning ch, turn.

Row 2: 3 ch (counts as 1 tr), (1 cluster, 2 ch and 1 cluster) into each ch sp to end, 1 tr

SHORT SCARF

Using 2.50 mm hook, make 59 ch.

Work foundation row as for Long Scarf.

14 patt repeats, 58 sts.

Beg with patt row 1, work in patt as for Long Scarf until work measures 115 cm (45¼ in), ending after patt row 2.

Do NOT fasten off.

Edging round: Working down adjacent row end edge, work 3 ch, 1 dc around tr at end of last row, *3 ch, 1 dc around 3 ch at beg of previous row, 3 ch, 1 dc around tr at end of previous row, rep from * until dc has been worked around tr at end of foundation row,

into top of turning ch, turn.

Rows 1 and 2 form patt.

Cont in patt until scarf measures 180 cm (71 in), ending after patt row 2.

Fasten off.

For fringe, cut 30 cm (12 in) lengths of yarn and knot pairs of threads across short ends of scarf, positioning each knot of fringe in corners of scarf and between each pair of clusters.

Do not press.

3 ch, 1 dc into same place as last dc, now working across foundation ch edge, work *3 ch, miss ch at base of clusters, (1 dc, 3 ch and 1 dc) into next ch sp, rep from * until both dc have been worked into ch sp at beg of foundation row, cont in this way until all four edges have been completed, replacing "dc" at end of last rep with "ss to first dc".

Fasten off.

Press lightly.

Working an Edging

Although the row ends of a piece of crochet can be very neat, they often look better if a separate edging is worked along them. This will smooth out the edge and create a more finished look.

When adding an edging to a piece of crochet, it is best to use a size or two smaller hook than the one used for the main sections. As the edging is there to hold the edge in shape and avoid it stretching, work it so that it just gently pulls the edge in slightly.

WORKING ACROSS THE TOP OF A ROW

When working across the top of a row of crochet, work the edging into the stitches in the same way as you would if working another row (**A**).

When working across the foundation chain edge, insert the hook under the remaining loop of each of the foundation chain stitches.

Depending on the stitch pattern being used for both the main section and the edging, you may find it necessary to either decrease or increase the number of stitches worked. As a crochet edging is very flexible, there is no real hard and fast rule as to how many stitches to work for an edging – the right number is the amount that sits properly. You

may find it easiest to try out the edging on your tension swatch to help work out the correct number of stitches you will need for the edging to sit correctly.

WORKING ALONG ROW ENDS

When working along row ends, place the stitches an even distance apart along the edge and the same distance in from the finished edge. Try to work the same number of stitches in each pair of row ends – as a guide, a double crochet edging worked along the sides of a treble fabric would need roughly three stitches for every two rows. Again, position the stitches so that they hold the edge in slightly (**B**).

If the edge is still wavy and too full after the first row or round of an edging has been completed, it will probably get worse once the rest of the edging has been worked! Take time at this point to unpick the first row or round and re-do it.

WORKING ALONG A CURVED EDGE

Working an edging along a curved edge will require varying numbers of stitches in each row, or round, to maintain a flat and smooth edging.

On an internal curve – such as a neck edge – work fewer stitches as required on each row or round by simply missing a stitch at even points along the edge (**C**).

On an external curve, you will need to add a few stitches to give the extra length needed. Do this by simply working twice into stitches as required (**D**).

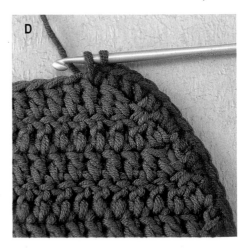

The amount of stitches you will need to add or lose will vary depending on how tight the curve is and the height of the stitch being used for the edging. Again, trial and error is the only sure-fire way of getting an edging to sit correctly.

Working an edging around a corner requires extra stitches to be added at the corner to allow the edging to turn without distorting the work (**E**).

E

As a guide, corners are normally turned by working three stitches into the actual corner point on most rows – but not all! Again, the number of times that extra stitches are added and how many are actually added will depend on the height of the stitch being used. You will obviously need more stitches to turn a corner with double trebles than with double crochet.

MAKING SEPARATE CROCHET EDGINGS

Crochet is also well suited to making a separate lacy edging that is sewn on to a ready-made item (**F**). These edgings can either be made lengthwise, working as long a length as required on a few stitches, or widthwise, by working just a few rows on the number of stitches needed to fit the edge.

Whichever way the edging is made, it is a good idea to make the edging slightly longer than it first appears to need to be. Crochet has a tendency to pull back in on itself and the edging therefore needs to have a little extra fullness to it. As a rough guide, add about an extra 5–10 cm (2–4 in) for every 100 cm (39½ in) of edging.

When calculating the amount of edging you need, remember to allow extra to turn any corners – you will need to add twice the finished width of the edging extra at each corner. And, if the edging is to go around a circular mat or cloth, remember to add extra so that the edging will lie flat. This extra length can be gently eased in as the edging is sewn in place. If possible, sew the edging in place as you make it, adding any extra length needed as you go along.

F

ATTACHING A CROCHET EDGING

Attaching a crochet edging to a ready-made item is best done by hand.

1. Place the edging and the item to be trimmed together, right sides facing, so that the inner (usually straight) edge of the edging matches the finished edge. Use a shade of sewing thread that complements the edging (we have used a contrasting colour here to illustrate the stitches) and very neatly slip stitch the inner edge of the edging in place to the outer edge of the item it is to trim. Work small, neat stitches, placing them close together so that the edging is securely held in place (**G**). Ease in any fullness as necessary as you stitch.

G

2. Once completed, fold the edging away from the item and press it carefully. The stitching, if worked correctly, should be virtually invisible.

Pressing

Once a piece of crochet has been completed, it should be pressed and the way in which this is done will vary, depending on the type of item being made and the yarn that has been used.

Remember – pressing is very different to ironing! When ironing, the iron slides around on the fabric surface. When pressing, the iron is gently lowered on to – or held just above – the fabric, held there for a second or two and then lifted away. It never slides over the surface.

Whatever yarn has been used, refer to the ball band to see how the manufacturer recommends that the yarn be pressed. Regardless of the directions given on the ball band, it is always a good idea to cover the

work with a pressing cloth to avoid any chance of damaging the surface of the work.

If the surface of the work is textured, sometimes it is better to simply block out the pieces, rather than press them. To block out a piece of crochet, you will need a flat, firm but soft surface that is larger than the crocheted piece – an ironing board or a table covered with soft towels is suitable.

Lay the crochet section on to this surface, with the right side uppermost, and gently ease the crochet into shape. Pin the edges

of the crochet in place, placing the pins at regular – but close – intervals along the edges. Make sure that you have pinned it square on to the surface and double check the size.

Once you are satisfied that everything is pinned in place, the crochet can be dampened. This can either be done by gently spraying with water from a laundry spray, or by covering the work with a damp cloth. Leave the pinned pieces in place to dry naturally before removing the cloth and pins. If necessary, the sections can then be joined to complete the work.

Circular lacy items that are supposed to lie flat are often nowhere near their finished size and are in no way flat when the crochet work has been completed. These items need to be pinned out on to a firm surface, stretching them to size. The design will often feature points around the outer edge – place the pins at these points to accentuate them. As a general rule, as the item is stretched to size, it will flatten out. If you are making a mat or cloth where the finished size is not vital and you cannot stretch it out to the specified size, simple adjust the pin positions so that the item is smooth at a comfortable size to show the stitches off well.

Once the item is stretched to size and pinned securely in place, it can either be pressed or blocked. Sometimes it may be necessary to use a combination of the two methods as pressing will help ease in any fullness stopping the centre from lying flat. If you want a fairly rigid crisp finish to the work, replace the water spray with spray starch. Whatever method is used, remember not to remove the pins until the item is completely dry.

Bedspread

Create your own heirloom with this traditional-style, cool white bedspread and add a touch of Victoriana to your home. It is made up of a number of squares joined together.

MEASUREMENTS

Finished single bedspread is 174 cm (68½ in) by 234 cm (92 in).
Finished double bedspread is 214 cm (84¼ in) by 234 cm (92 in).

MATERIALS

Rowan Handknit DK Cotton in white (Bleached 263) – you will need 84 x 50 g balls for single size, or 104 x 50 g balls for double size
3.50 mm (UK 9/USA E4) crochet hook

TENSION

One square measures 20 cm (8 in) using 3.50 mm hook, or size required to give correct tension.

ABBREVIATIONS

popcorn = work 5 tr into same place, take hook out of working loop, insert it through top of first of these 5 tr, pick up working loop again and draw through top of first tr to close top of popcorn – ensure popcorn projects out on to right side of work.
See also page 11.

SQUARE

Using 3.50 mm hook, make 6 ch and join with a ss to form a ring.
Round 1: 3 ch, 4 tr into ring, take hook out of working loop, insert it through top of 3 ch at beg of round, pick up working loop again and draw through top of 3 ch to close top of starting popcorn, (5 ch, 1 popcorn into ring) 3 times, 5 ch, ss to top of starting popcorn.
Round 2: 3 ch (counts as 1 tr), *(2 tr, 2 ch, 1 popcorn, 2 ch and 2 tr) into next ch sp**,

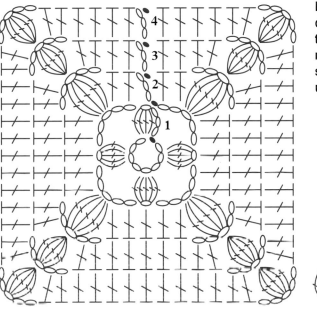

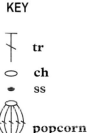

KEY

T	tr
⬭	ch
・	ss
popcorn symbol	popcorn

LEFT: This stitch diagram shows the first four rounds of each square that makes up the bedspread.

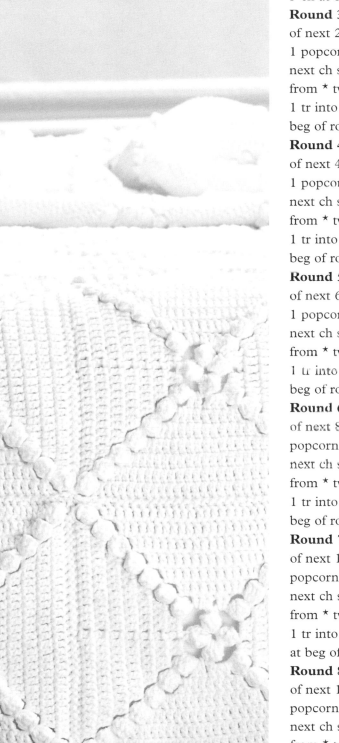

1 tr into next popcorn, rep from * twice more, then from * to ** again, ss to top of 3 ch at beg of round.

Round 3: 3 ch (counts as 1 tr), 1 tr into each of next 2 tr, *2 tr into next ch sp, 2 ch, 1 popcorn into next popcorn, 2 ch, 2 tr into next ch sp**, 1 tr into each of next 5 tr, rep from * twice more, then from * to ** again, 1 tr into each of next 2 tr, ss to top of 3 ch at beg of round.

Round 4: 3 ch (counts as 1 tr), 1 tr into each of next 4 tr, *2 tr into next ch sp, 2 ch, 1 popcorn into next popcorn, 2 ch, 2 tr into next ch sp**, 1 tr into each of next 9 tr, rep from * twice more, then from * to ** again, 1 tr into each of next 4 tr, ss to top of 3 ch at beg of round.

Round 5: 3 ch (counts as 1 tr), 1 tr into each of next 6 tr, *2 tr into next ch sp, 2 ch, 1 popcorn into next popcorn, 2 ch, 2 tr into next ch sp**, 1 tr into each of next 13 tr, rep from * twice more, then from * to ** again, 1 tr into each of next 6 tr, ss to top of 3 ch at beg of round.

Round 6: 3 ch (counts as 1 tr), 1 tr into each of next 8 tr, *2 tr into next ch sp, 2 ch, 1 popcorn into next popcorn, 2 ch, 2 tr into next ch sp**, 1 tr into each of next 17 tr, rep from * twice more, then from * to ** again, 1 tr into each of next 8 tr, ss to top of 3 ch at beg of round.

Round 7: 3 ch (counts as 1 tr), 1 tr into each of next 10 tr, *2 tr into next ch sp, 2 ch, 1 popcorn into next popcorn, 2 ch, 2 tr into next ch sp**, 1 tr into each of next 21 tr, rep from * twice more, then from * to ** again, 1 tr into each of next 10 tr, ss to top of 3 ch at beg of round.

Round 8: 3 ch (counts as 1 tr), 1 tr into each of next 12 tr, *2 tr into next ch sp, 2 ch, 1 popcorn into next popcorn, 2 ch, 2 tr into next ch sp**, 1 tr into each of next 25 tr, rep from * twice more, then from * to ** again, 1 tr into each of next 12 tr, ss to top of 3 ch at beg of round.
Fasten off.
Completed square has a popcorn in each corner, 2 ch on each side of this popcorn and 29 tr along sides between corners.

CENTRE SECTION

For a single bedspread, make 88 squares. For a double bedspread, make 110 squares. Join squares to form Centre Section as follows: Hold two squares together with right sides facing and work a row of dc along the joining edge, working 1 dc for each popcorn, ch or tr and inserting hook for each dc through top of relevant st on both squares. Fasten off. Join squares to form 11 strips of 8 squares for single bedspread, or 10 squares for double bedspread, then join strips to form a rectangle 11 squares long by 8 squares wide for single bedspread, or 10 squares wide for double bedspread.

EDGING

Using 3.50 mm hook, rejoin yarn at one point where squares have been joined and, with right side facing, work edging all round

Centre Section as follows:

Round 1: 3 ch, 4 tr into joining point, take hook out of working loop, insert it through top of 3 ch at beg of round, pick up working loop again and draw through top of 3 ch to close top of starting popcorn, *1 ch, miss 2 ch, 1 tr into each of next 13 tr, 1 ch, miss 1 tr, 1 popcorn into next tr, 1 ch, miss 1 tr, 1 tr into each of next 13 tr, 1 ch, miss 2 ch, 1 popcorn into next joining point, rep from * to end, working popcorn into corner popcorns at all four corners of Centre Section and omitting popcorn at end of last rep, ss to top of starting popcorn.

Now work each point of Edging separately.

Row 2: 3 ch, miss popcorn at base of 3 ch and next 1 ch, 1 popcorn into next tr, 1 ch, miss 1 tr, 1 tr into each of next 9 tr, 1 ch, miss 1 tr, 1 popcorn into next tr, miss 1 ch, 1 tr into top of next popcorn (mark this

popcorn), turn.

Row 3 – 3 ch, miss first popcorn and next 1 ch, 1 popcorn into next tr, 1 ch, miss 1 tr, 1 tr into each of next 5 tr, 1 ch, miss 1 tr, 1 popcorn into next tr, miss 1 ch, 1 tr into top of next popcorn, turn.

Row 4: 3 ch, miss first popcorn and next 1 ch, 1 popcorn into next tr, 1 ch, miss 1 tr, 1 tr into next tr, 1 ch, miss 1 tr, 1 popcorn into next tr, miss 1 ch, 1 tr into top of next popcorn, turn.

Row 5: 3 ch, miss first popcorn and next 1 ch, 1 popcorn into next tr, miss 1 ch, 1 tr into top of next popcorn.

Fasten off.

First point of Edging completed.

With right side facing, re-join yarn to marked popcorn and work rows 2 to 5 again.

Continue in this way until points have been worked all round Centre Section.

With right side facing, re-join yarn to outer edge and work one round of dc all round points of Edging, working 3 dc into each 3 ch sp along sides of points and 1 dc into popcorn at top of point, and ending with ss to first dc, do NOT turn.

Now work one round of crab stitch (dc worked from left to right, not right to left) around entire outer edge, ending with ss to first dc.

Fasten off.

To Finish

Carefully press from wrong side, using a warm iron over a damp cloth. Work on a soft but firm surface (such as several layers of towels laid over an ironing board). Once complete, gently ease any popcorns that may have slipped through to the wrong side back through to the right side of the work.

Edging

Enhance sheets and pillow slips with this simple but effective lacy edging. Quick and easy to crochet, this edging can be made to any length required.

MEASUREMENTS

Finished edging is approx 3 cm (1¼ in) wide

MATERIALS

Coats Aida 5 Crochet Cotton in white (colour 1) – one 50 g ball will be sufficient for approx 260 cm (102 in) of edging
1.75 mm (UK 15/USA 5 steel) crochet hook

TENSION

One pattern repeat (4 rows) measures 2.5 cm (1 in) using 1.75 mm hook, or size required to give correct tension.

ABBREVIATIONS

See page 11.

EDGING

Using 1.75 mm hook, make 6 ch.

Foundation row: 1 tr into 4th ch from hook, 1 tr into each of next 2 ch, turn. 4 sts.

Now work in patt as follows:

Row 1: 3 ch (counts as 1 tr), miss first st, 1 tr into each of rem 3 sts, working last tr into top of turning ch, turn.

Row 2: As row 1.

Row 3: 3 ch (counts as 1 tr), miss first st, 1 tr into each of next 2 tr, (1 tr – mark this tr, 4 ch and 1 dc) into top of turning ch, 7 ch, working along row end edges 1 dc into same place as last tr of row 1, 2 ch, 1 tr into corresponding point along row edge but one row lower, turn.

Row 4: Miss (1 tr, 2 ch and 1 dc), [1 ch, 1 tr into next ch sp] 6 times, 1 ch, miss 1 dc, 1 dc into next ch sp, ss along and into marked tr,

3 ch (counts as 1 tr), 1 tr into each of rem 3 sts, working last tr into top of turning ch, turn.

These 4 rows form patt.

Cont in patt until Edging is required length, ending after patt row 3.

Next row: Miss (1 tr, 2 ch and 1 dc), [1 ch, 1 tr into next ch sp] 6 times, 1 ch, miss 1 dc, 1 dc into next ch sp, turn.

Along edge of each scallop there are 9 ch sps – work into these ch sps for the edging row.

Now work along outer edge of scallops as follows:

Edging row: Miss dc at end of last row, *[1 dc into next ch sp, 4 ch] 6 times, 1 dc into next ch sp (this is 8th ch sp of this scallop)**, 1 ch, miss last ch sp of this scallop and first ch sp of next scallop, rep from * to end, ending last rep at **.

Fasten off.

To Make Up

Press carefully. Pin edging in place to fabric edges, then neatly sew straight edge to outer edge of fabric, gathering edging to fit around corners, joining ends of edging if necessary.

Baby Cardigan, Hat and Blanket

The pretty, textured flowers make this adorable baby jacket, hat and blanket extra special. Choose soft pastel colours for your new arrival.

MEASUREMENTS

To fit age	0-3	3-6	6-12	12-18 months
Chest	41	46	51	56 cm
	16	18	20	22 in

CARDIGAN

Actual size	47	52	57	62 cm
	18½	20½	22½	24½ in
Length	21	25	29	33 cm
	8¼	10	11½	13 in
Sleeve seam	13	16	20	26 cm
	5	6¼	8	10¼ in

HAT

Width around head	30	35	35	40 cm
	12	13¾	13¾	15¾ in

BLANKET

Finished size	69 x 89 cm
	27 x 35 in

MATERIALS

Sirdar Country Style 4 ply (50 g balls):

For cardigan and hat:

MS – white	1	1	2	2 balls
A – pink	1	1	1	1 balls
B – blue	1	1	1	1 balls

2.50 mm (UK 12/USA C2) crochet hook
4 buttons

For blanket:

MS – white	6 balls
A – pink	3 balls
B – blue	3 balls

2.50 mm (UK 12/USA C2) crochet hook

TENSION

23 sts and 12½ rows to 10 cm (4 in) measured over treble fabric using 2.50 mm hook, or size required to give correct tension. Motif measures 5 cm (2 in) square.

ABBREVIATIONS

tr2tog = *yoh and insert into next st, yoh and draw loop through, yoh and draw through 2 loops, rep from * once more, yoh and draw through all 3 loops on hook.
See also page 11.

FLOWER MOTIF

Using 2.50 mm hook and first colour (either pink or blue), make 5 ch and join with a ss to form a ring.
Round 1: *2 ch, (4 tr and 1 ss) into ring, rep from * twice more.
Round 2: Working behind petals of round 1, miss 2 ch at beg of previous round, 1 dc into

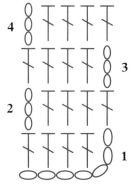

LEFT: This stitch diagram shows the treble fabric used for the main sections of the cardigan and hat.

KEY

	tr
	ch

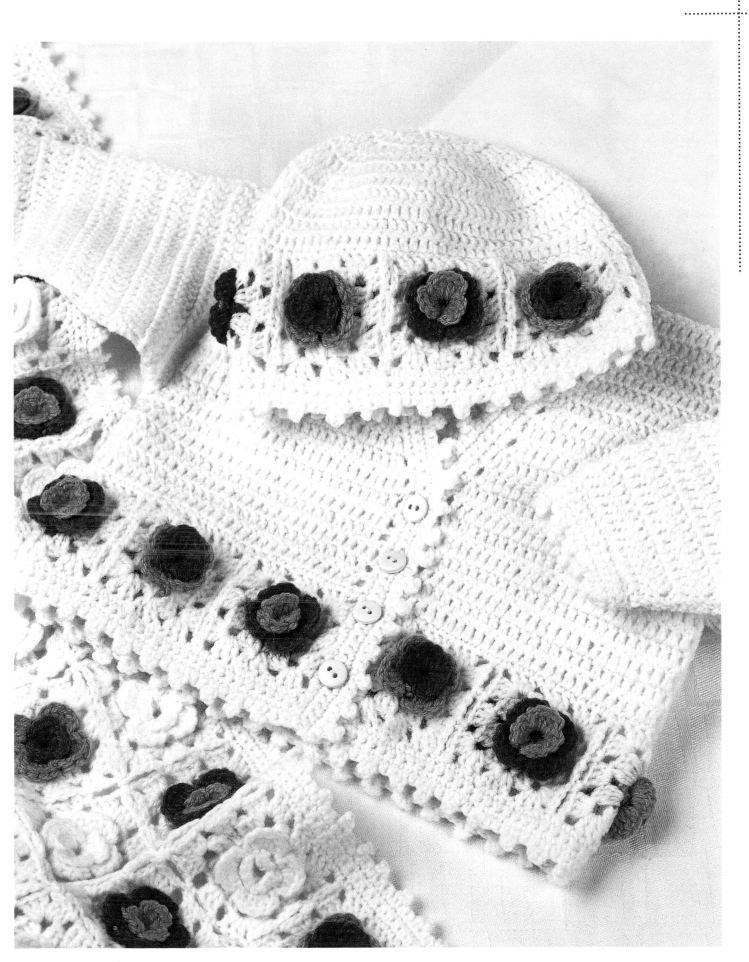

foundation ring, 2 ch, miss 3 tr, 1 dc into ring, 2 ch, miss (1 tr, 1 ss, 2 ch and 2 tr), 1 dc into foundation ring, 2 ch, miss (2 tr, 1 ss, 2 ch and 1 tr), 1 dc into foundation ring, 2 ch, miss (3 tr and 1 ss), ss to first dc.

Break off first colour and join in second colour.

Round 3: (1 ss, 5 tr and 1 ss) into each ch sp of previous round.

Round 4: Working behind petals of round 3, 1 ch, *inserting hook from back and from right to left work 1 dc around stem of dc of round 2, 4 ch, rep from * 3 times more, ss to first dc.

Break off second colour and join in MS.

Round 5: Ss into first ch sp, 3 ch (counts as first tr), (2 tr, 3 ch and 3 tr) into same ch sp, *1 ch, (3 tr, 3 ch and 3 tr) into next ch sp, rep from * twice more, 1 dc into 3rd of 3 ch at beg of round.

Round 6: 3 ch (counts as first tr), 2 tr into sp formed by dc at end of previous round, *1 ch, (3 tr, 3 ch and 3 tr) into next ch sp, 1 ch**, 3 tr into next ch sp, rep from * twice more and then from * to ** again, ss to 3rd of 3 ch at beg of round.

Fasten off.

Each motif is a square and has one 3 ch sp in each corner and two 1 ch sps along each side. The motifs are joined to form the final pieces whilst working round 6. Replace the (3 ch) at each corner with (1 ch, 1 dc into corresponding corner sp on Motif to be joined, 1 ch), and the (1 ch) along sides with (1 dc into corresponding 1 ch sp on Motif to be joined).

CARDIGAN

BODY (worked in one piece to armholes)

Motif Border

Make and join a strip of 9 [10:11:12] Motifs as follows: use A as first colour and B as second colour on First Motif, B as first colour and A as second colour on Second Motif, and cont in this way, alternating colours at centres.

Hem Border

With RS facing, using 2.50 mm hook and MS, work 103 [115:127:139] dc evenly along lower edge of Motif Border (this is 11 dc for each motif plus an extra 4 [5:6:7] dc evenly distributed along edge), turn.

Row 1: (WS), 1 ch (does NOT count as st), 1 dc into each dc to end, turn.

Row 2: As row 1.

Row 3: 1 ch (does NOT count as st), 1 dc into each of first 2 dc, *3 ch, ss to top of last dc, 1 dc into each of next 3 dc, rep from * to last 2 dc, 3 ch, ss to top of last dc, 1 dc into each of last 2 dc.

Fasten off.

Main Section

With RS facing, using 2.50 mm hook and MS, work 103 [115:127:139] dc evenly along upper edge of Motif Border (this is 11 dc for each motif plus an extra 4 [5:6:7] dc evenly distributed along edge), turn.

Row 1: 3 ch (counts as first st), 1 tr into each st to end, turn.

This row forms treble fabric.

Cont in treble fabric until Main Section measures 10 [13:16:19] cm from lower edge.

Divide for armholes

Next row: 3 ch (counts as first st), tr2tog over next 2 sts, 1 tr into each of next 22 [25:28:31] tr, turn.

Work on this set of 24 [27:30:33] sts only for first front.

Next row: 3 ch (counts as first st), 1 tr into each tr to last 3 sts, tr2tog over next 2 sts, 1 tr into last st, turn.

Working all decreases as set by last 2 rows, dec 1 st at front slope edge of next 3 [4:5:6] rows, then on every foll alt row until 17 [19:21:23] sts rem.

Work a few rows straight until armhole measures 11 [12:13:14] cm.

Fasten off.

Shape back

Return to last complete row worked, rejoin yarn to next tr with RS facing and proceed as follows:

Next row: 3 ch (counts as first st), 1 tr into each of next 52 [58:64:70] tr, turn.

Cont on these 53 [59:65:71] sts only until

back matches first front to shoulder.
Fasten off.

Shape second front

Return to last complete row worked, rejoin
yarn to next tr with RS facing and proceed as
follows:

Next row – 3 ch (counts as first st), 1 tr into
each tr to last 3 sts, tr2tog over next 2 sts,
1 tr into last st, turn.

Complete second front to match first,
reversing shapings.

SLEEVES

Main Section

Using 2.50 mm hook and MS, make
31 [33:35:37] ch.

Row 1: 1 tr into 4th ch from hook, 1 tr into
each ch to end, turn. 29 [31:33:35] sts.

Row 2: 3 ch (counts as first st), 2 tr into next
tr, 1 tr into tr to last 2 sts, 2 tr into next st,
1 tr into last st, turn. 31 [33:35:37] sts.

Working all increases as set by last row, inc
1 st at each end of next 10 [10:6:1] rows,
then on foll 0 [1:6:12] alt rows.
51 [55:59:63] sts.

Work a few rows straight until Sleeve
measures 11 [14:18:24] cm.

Fasten off.

Cuff

With RS facing, using 2.50 mm hook and
MS, work 28 [31:34:34] dc evenly along

foundation ch edge of Sleeve, turn.
Work rows 1 to 3 as given for Hem Border of
Body.
Fasten off.

TO MAKE UP
Join shoulder seams.
Front and Neck Edging
Mark positions for 4 buttonholes along right
front opening edge – top button level with
start of front slope shaping, lowest buttonhole
1 cm (½ in) above lower edge and rem 2
buttonholes evenly spaced between.
With RS facing, using 2.50 mm hook and
MS, rejoin yarn at base of right front opening
edge and, working a multiple of 3 sts, work a
row of dc up right front opening edge to
shoulder, across back neck and down left
front opening edge to lower edge, turn.
Row 1: (WS), 1 ch (does NOT count as st),
1 dc into each dc to end, making buttonholes
to correspond with positions marked for

buttonholes by replacing (1 dc into each of
next 2 dc) with (2 ch, miss 2 dc) and working
2 dc into dc at corner points at beg of front
slope shaping, turn.
Row 2: 1 ch (does NOT count as st), 1 dc
into each dc to end, working 2 dc into each
buttonhole ch sp, turn.
Row 3: 1 ch (does NOT count as st), 1 dc
into first dc, ★3 ch, ss to top of last dc, 1 dc
into each of next 3 dc, rep from ★ to last dc,
3 ch, ss to top of last dc, 1 dc into last dc.
Fasten off.
Join sleeve seams. Sew sleeves into armholes.
Sew on buttons.

HAT
Motif Border
Make and join a strip of 6 [7:7:8] Motifs as
follows: use A as first colour and B as second
colour on First Motif, B as first colour and A
as second colour on Second Motif, and cont
in this way, alternating colours at centres.

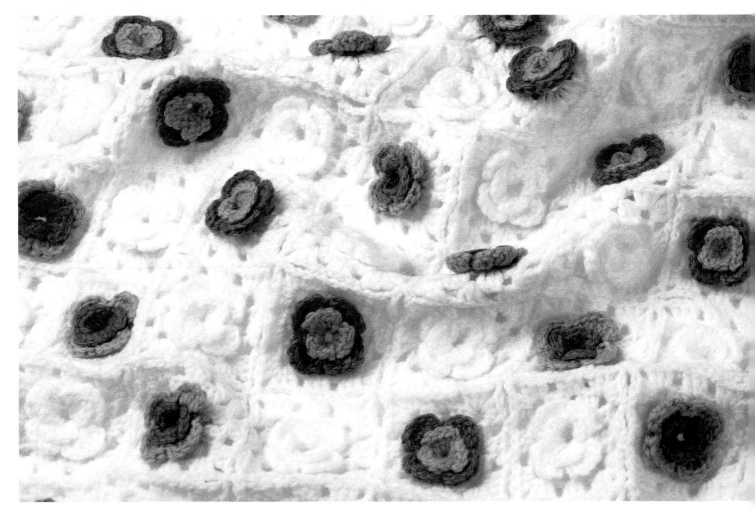

Hem Border

With RS facing, using 2.50 mm hook and MS, work 67 [79:79:91] dc evenly along lower edge of Motif Border (this is 11 dc for each motif plus an extra 1 [2:2:3] evenly distributed along edge dc), turn.

Row 1: (WS), 1 ch (does NOT count as st), 1 dc into each dc to end, turn.

Row 2: As row 1.

Row 3: 1 ch (does NOT count as st), 1 dc into each of first 2 dc, *3 ch, ss to top of last dc, 1 dc into each of next 3 dc, rep from * to last 2 dc, 3 ch, ss to top of last dc, 1 dc into each of last 2 dc.

Fasten off.

Main Section

With RS facing, using 2.50 mm hook and MS, work 67 [78:78:89] dc evenly along upper edge of Motif Border (this is 11 dc for each motif plus an extra 1 dc), turn.

Row 1: 3 ch (counts as first st), 1 tr into each st to end, turn.

This row forms treble fabric.

Cont in treble fabric until Main Section measures 9 [10:11:12] cm from lower edge.

Shape crown

Row 1: 3 ch (counts as first st), (tr2tog over next 2 sts, 1 tr into each of next 9 tr) 6 [7:7:8] times, turn. 61 [71:71:81] sts.

Row 2: 3 ch (counts as first st), (tr2tog over next 2 sts, 1 tr into each of next 3 tr) 12 [14:14:16] times, turn. 49 [57:57:65] sts.

Row 3: 3 ch (counts as first st), (tr2tog over next 2 sts, 1 tr into each of next 2 tr) 12 [14:14:16] times, turn. 37 [43:43:49] sts.

Row 4: 3 ch (counts as first st), (tr2tog over next 2 sts, 1 tr into next tr) 12 [14:14:16] times, turn. 25 [29:29:33] sts.

Row 5: 3 ch (counts as first st), (tr2tog over next 2 sts) 12 [14:14:16] times, turn. 13 [15:15:17] sts.

Row 6: 3 ch (counts as first st), (tr2tog over

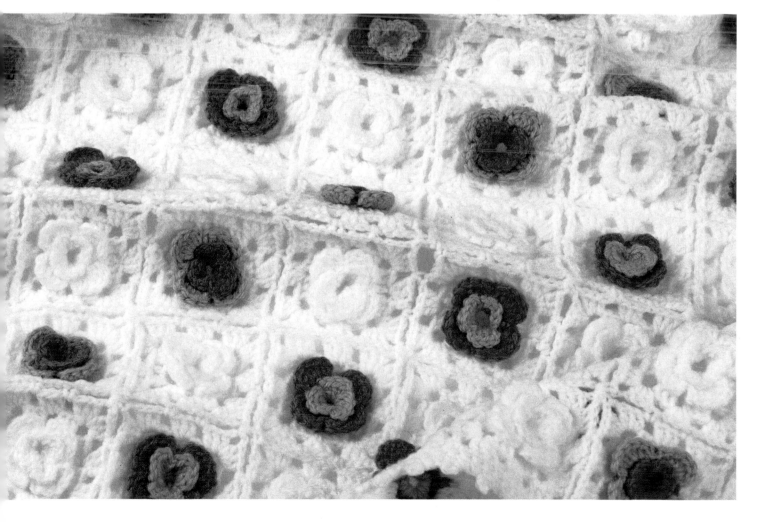

RIGHT: Follow this chart for the correct positioning of the motifs on the baby blanket.

A	B	A	C	A	B	A	B	A	C	A	B	A
B	A	C	A	B	A	C	A	B	A	C	A	B
A	C	A	B	A	C	A	C	A	B	A	C	A
C	A	B	A	C	A	B	A	C	A	B	A	C
A	B	A	C	A	B	A	B	A	C	A	B	A
B	A	C	A	B	A	C	A	B	A	C	A	B
A	C	A	B	A	C	A	C	A	B	A	C	A
C	A	B	A	C	A	B	A	C	A	B	A	C
A	B	A	C	A	B	A	B	A	C	A	B	A
C	A	B	A	C	A	B	A	C	A	B	A	C
A	C	A	B	A	C	A	C	A	B	A	C	A
B	A	C	A	B	A	C	A	B	A	C	A	B
A	B	A	C	A	B	A	B	A	C	A	B	A
C	A	B	A	C	A	B	A	C	A	B	A	C
A	C	A	B	A	C	A	C	A	B	A	C	A
B	A	C	A	B	A	C	A	B	A	C	A	B
A	B	A	C	A	B	A	B	A	C	A	B	A

A = work all rounds of motif using Main Shade

B = use A as 1st colour, B as 2nd colour and work rest of motif in Main Shade

C = use B as 1st colour, A as 2nd colour and work rest of motif in Main Shade

next 2 sts) 6 [7:7:8] times, turn. 7 [8:8:9] sts.
Fasten off.
Join back seam.

BLANKET
Main Section
Make and join 221 Motifs to form a rectangle
13 motifs wide by 17 motifs long, using
colours as indicated on diagram opposite.

Border
With RS facing, using 2.50 mm hook and
MS, work 1 row of dc evenly all round outer
edge of Main Section, working 11 dc along
sides of each motif and an extra 1 dc in each
corner, ss to first dc, turn. 664 sts.
Round 1: (WS), 1 ch (does NOT count as st),
1 dc into each dc to end, working 3 dc into
each corner dc and ending with ss to first
dc, turn. 672 sts.
Round 2: As round 1. 680 sts.
Round 3: 1 ch (does NOT count as st),
1 dc into first dc, *3 ch, ss to top of last dc,
1 dc into each of next 3 dc, rep from * to
last dc, 3 ch, ss to top of last dc, 1 dc into
last dc, ss to first dc.
Fasten off.

To Finish
Carefully press from wrong side, using a
cool iron over a dry cloth. Work on a soft
but firm surface (such as several layers of
towels laid over an ironing board). Gently
ease the flowers of each motif into shape.

Placing the Stitches

The textured effects that appear in crochet are formed in a variety of ways. They can either be made by working the basic stitches in combinations that create the texture, or they can be created by varying the point where the base of the stitch is placed.

When creating a textured effect by varying the placement of the stitches, the actual stitch being worked will be made in exactly the same way as would normally be the case – it is only the point where the hook is inserted through the previous rows or rounds that changes. Check the pattern you are following to find out exactly how to place the stitches.

WORKING INTO THE TOPS OF STITCHES

This is the most usual way to place a stitch – it is worked by inserting the hook from the front under both loops of the "V" at the top of the stitch being worked (**A**). This is the standard way to insert the hook for all the basic crochet stitches and all stitches should be worked in this manner unless the pattern specifies otherwise. The only time a pattern may specify to work a stitch in this way is after they have been worked differently, to point out that the normal placement of stitches should now be used.

A

WORKING THROUGH ONE LOOP

By working the new stitches through just one of the loops of the "V", a line is left across the work (**B**). This line forms a slight ridge and, by alternating which loop is left unworked – either the front or back loop – a basket-weave effect can be created.

B

When working in rows, working into the same (front or back) loop of every stitch of every row with leave a ridge on the front of the work for one row and at the back of the work for the next row. If you want the ridges to appear on one particular side for every row, the loop used for the stitch must be alternated – for example, use the front loop for all right side rows and the back loop for every wrong side row.

Similarly, when working in rounds, working into the same (front or back) loop for every round will leave the ridge on the same side of

the work throughout. If the ridge is to alternately appear on both sides of the work then the loop used for the stitch must be alternated on every round.

WORKING INTO CHAIN SPACES

1. Placing the new stitches into a chain space (**abbreviated to "ch sp"**), rather than working into the actual chain stitches, completely encloses the chain. The stitches are worked in the normal way but, instead of inserting the hook under the two bars of the "V", it is inserted into the chain space (**C**).

C

Rarely will you find the same number of stitches worked into a chain space as there are chain making up the space. Many lacy patterns will work just one stitch into a chain space, to create a mesh effect, or many stitches, to shape the work or form a particular stitch group.

WORKING BETWEEN STITCHES

Placing the new stitches between the stitches of a previous row, or round, will create a slightly lacy effect as the stitches of the previous row are gently eased apart.

Insert the hook from the front, taking great care to insert the hook between the stitches without accidentally picking up a strand of one of them (**D**).

D

A stitch worked in this way will add less height to the work than one worked into the top of a row or round. This is because the base of the stitch is below the top of the previous row.

RELIEF STITCHES

Instead of working into a stitch, it is possible to work around the body of the stitch, between the point where it joins the previous row and the top where the "V" will be visible. Because of the heavily textured effect this creates, this type of stitch is known as a relief stitch. Although, within reason, it is possible to work any height of relief stitch, a relief treble is the most commonly used type.

Relief stitches create very heavily textured fabrics that can be reversible. The crochet stitches are also quite tightly packed on each other so a lot of yarn is used –- but they form a thick, warm fabric that is ideal for outer-wear, and blankets and throws.

To work a relief front treble (**abbreviated to "rftr"**), wrap the yarn around the hook and then insert it from the front and from the right to the left around the stem of the stitch of the previous row. Wrap the yarn around the hook in the usual way and draw this loop through from the beginning of the stem of the stitch being worked (**E**). Now complete the treble in the normal way.

E

To work a relief back treble (**abbreviated to "rbtr"**), wrap the yarn around the hook and insert the hook into the work from the back and from the right to the left around the stem of the stitch of the previous row. Wrap the yarn around the hook in the normal way and draw this new loop through the work (**F**). Complete the stitch in the usual way.

F

Because the base of a relief stitch is below the top of the previous row, a relief stitch is shorter than its "normal" version. It is therefore necessary to reduce the length of the turning chain accordingly. A fabric made up of relief treble stitches would use a turning chain of just two chain, rather than the usual three.

As the first row of relief stitches requires the stitches of the previous row to have sufficient height to be able to work around their stems, this foundation row needs to be fairly tall. A fabric that used relief treble stitches would normally be worked on to a foundation row of half treble stitches.

Baby Blankets

Keep little ones cosy in their prams or buggies with these warm blankets in soft pastel shades.

MEASUREMENTS
Finished blanket is 75 cm (29½ in) by 100 cm (39½ in)

MATERIALS
For striped blanket:
Sirdar Wash 'n' Wear Double Crepe:
8 x 50 g balls in first colour (white), and
8 x 50 g balls in second colour (blue)
For plain blanket:
Sirdar Wash 'n' Wear Double Crepe:
15 x 50 g balls in yellow
For both blankets:
3.50 mm (UK 9/USA E4) crochet hook

TENSION
20 sts and 11 rows to 10 cm (4 in) measured over pattern using 3.50 mm hook, or size required to give correct tension.

ABBREVIATIONS
rftr = relief front treble worked as follows: work treble in usual way around stem of next st by inserting hook around stem of stitch from front and from right to left.
See also page 11.

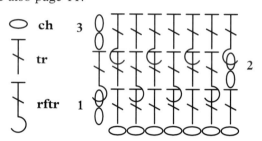

LEFT: In this stitch diagram the "hook" at the base of the treble stitch symbol signifies a relief stitch. Although all the relief stitches are relief front trebles, the symbol is reversed for every other row as the direction of the work is also reversed.

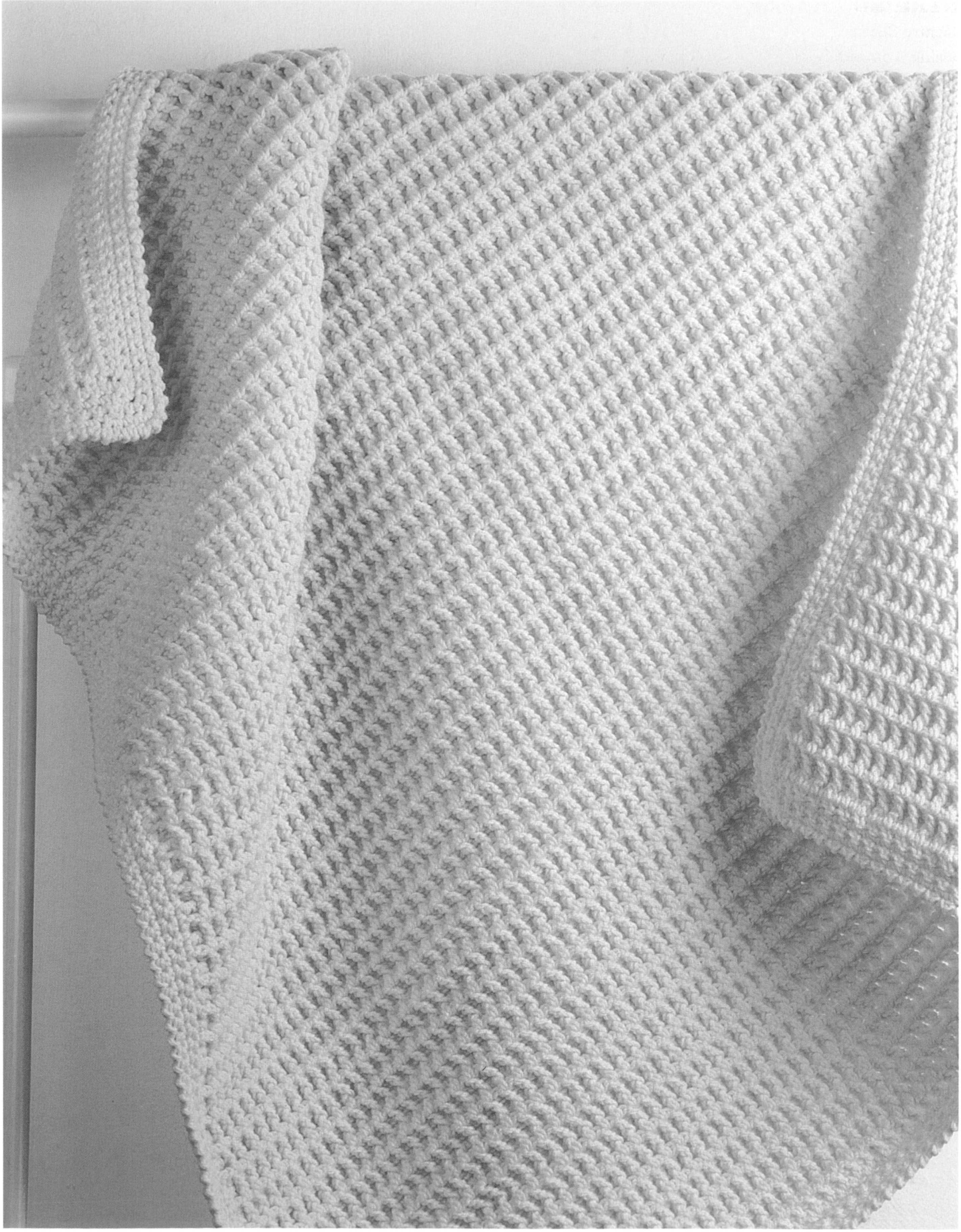

STRIPED BLANKET

Centre Section

Using 3.50 mm hook and first colour, make 145 ch.

Foundation row: 1 tr into 3rd ch from hook, 1 tr into each ch to end, turn. 144 sts.

Row 1: 2 ch (counts as first st), * 1 rftr around next st, 1 tr into next st, rep from * to last st, 1 rftr around turning ch, turn.

This row forms patt.

Work a further 7 rows in patt using first colour.

**Break off first colour and join in second colour.

Using second colour, work in patt for 8 rows.

Break off second colour and join in first colour.

Using first colour, work in patt for 8 rows.

Rep from ** 5 times more.

Break off first colour and join in second colour.

Work should measure 96 cm (37¾ in).

Edging

Using second colour throughout, work edging as folls:

Round 1: 1 ch (does NOT count as st), now work 1 round of dc around all four edges, working 1 dc into each st across top of last row and across foundation ch edge, 3 dc into each corner point, and 3 dc into each pair of row end edges along sides, ending with ss to first dc, turn.

Round 2: 1 ch (does NOT count as st), 1 dc into each dc to end, working 3 dc into corner dc and ending with ss to first dc, turn.

Rounds 3 and 4: As round 2.

Now work 1 round of crab st (dc worked from left to right, instead of right to left) around entire outer edge, ending with ss to first st.

Fasten off.

PLAIN BLANKET

Work as given for two coloured blanket but using same colour throughout.

Filet Crochet

Filet crochet is the name given to a particular type of crochet that forms a mesh fabric, made up of tiny open or solid crochet squares.

Normally worked following a chart, this chart is an accurate reflection of what the finished crochet will look like. The chart will feature solid blocks and open squares, arranged to form any type of design – geometric, floral, pictorial or even spelling out words. The resulting fabric can be densely filled with a solid design, or very open creating a mesh with little design on it (see chart below).

Worked in a fine yarn, filet crochet generally uses just chain stitches and trebles. The grid of the chart directly relates to the mesh of the crochet. Each row of squares on the chart becomes one row of the crochet. Each

vertical line dividing the chart squares is worked as one treble stitch. Each horizontal line on the chart is a group of chain stitches.

As the blocks of the crochet mesh should be true squares, each block is most often made up of three or four chains or treble stitches. There will be a treble at each side of the square, forming the vertical outline of the mesh, and either two chain or two treble stitches between, to either create the mesh or fill in the square. There are, of course, exceptions to this rule – check the pattern you are following to make sure you know what size the mesh is supposed to be!

WORKING THE FILET MESH

1. Start a piece of filet crochet by making a foundation chain of the required length – this will be detailed in the pattern. Now work the first row of stitches that form the first row of squares by working into this chain.
2. To create a mesh fabric, work each square by working a treble at each side of the square and two chain to run across the top. The lower, fourth side of the square has already been formed by the foundation chain or, later on, by previous rows (**A**).

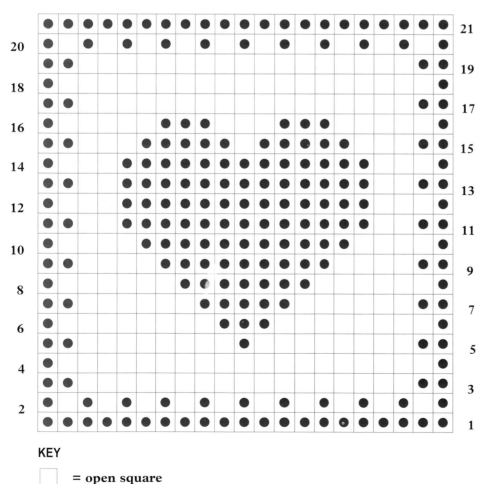

LEFT: This simple heart design, worked in filet crochet, is made up of solid blocks to form the heart motif on a mesh of open squares, with a border of solid squares. On this chart the solid squares are shown as a solid dot inside the square of the mesh, but you will sometimes find the solid square represented as a solid, filled-in black square. There are no details with the key to this diagram as to how to work the mesh so you would need to refer to the written instructions for this. The rows of the design are numbered and the numbers appear at the beginning of each row.

KEY

☐ = open square

⊙ = solid block

3. To fill in a square of the chart – to create a "block" – replace the two chain that would have formed the upper side of the square with two trebles stitches worked into the chain running across the bottom of the square. The two treble stitches can either be worked into the chain stitches below them, or into the chain space (**B**). The effect created is very similar – but working into the chain space is much easier!

Remember that at the beginning of a row of filet crochet there will be a turning chain. Once the treble has been worked at the end of one row, turn the work and work the three chain that are needed to replace the treble that needs to sit at the beginning of the next row.

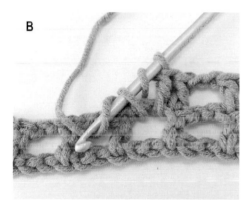

B

If the edge square of the design is an open square, you need to work a further two chain to create the top of the square – a total of five chain. When working back over this open end square, remember to work the last treble into the third of these five chain. If the edge square of the design is a solid block, you will need to work the two trebles that fill the block. If the square below is an open square, work these into the chain or chain space across the top. If the square below is a solid block, work one treble into each of the two trebles that form the block below.

Although filet crochet is usually worked flat, in rows, it can be worked in rounds. Start each round in the same way as you would if working a row, and close each round by working a slip stitch into the top of the three chain at the beginning of the round. Although there is no need to turn the work at the end

of each round, when working a circular piece of filet crochet it is a good idea. The trebles that form the vertical lines of the grid mesh tend to lean to one side slightly and, if all trebles lean one way, the finished work will have a tendency to twist and bias.

Although most filet crochet designs are made up of simple open and solid squares, or "blocks", there are a few common variations.

LACETS AND BARS
Both of these "design details" usually appear together and fill two squares on the chart or mesh.

1. To work a lacet, start by working the treble at the beginning of a square. Now replace the next two treble or chain stitches with a diagonal line of three chain stitches. Complete the "square" by working a double crochet into the point where the final treble should have been placed. To continue the lacet, work another diagonal line of three chain to replace the next two stitches, and complete the lacet by working a treble into the normal place to form the last vertical side of the two squares. The resulting lacet forms a lacy "V" that sits over two squares of the mesh (**C**).

C

2. When working back over a lacet, it is necessary to work a bar that covers the top of both squares. A single open square will have a treble at each side and two chain across the top. For a double bar to cover a lacet, you will need to work five chain at the centre – two for each "square" and one to replace the missing centre treble. Remember when working back over a bar that you will usually need to work a treble into the third of these five chain (**D**).

D

When following a chart for filet crochet, take time to read the key accompanying the chart, as well as any special abbreviations, so that you fully understand how the grid mesh is formed and how to work any details.

Filet Curtain Panel

Hide an ugly view with this pretty filet crochet panel set into a piece of sheer white fabric. Why not make a second panel and use it as a pretty table cloth?

MEASUREMENTS

Finished panel is approx 52 cm (20½ in) wide and 30 cm (12 in) tall.

MATERIALS

2 x 50 g balls of Coats Aida 5 Crochet Cotton in white
1.75 mm (UK 15/USA 5 steel) crochet hook

TENSION

14 blocks and 17 rows to 10 cm (4 in) using 1.75 mm hook, or size required to give correct tension.

ABBREVIATIONS

See page 11.

PANEL

Using 1.75 mm hook, make 222 ch.

Row 1: 1 tr into 4th ch from hook, 1 tr into each ch to end, turn. 220 sts.

Row 2: 3 ch (counts as 1 tr), miss tr at end of last row, 1 tr into each of next 3 tr, *2 ch, miss 2 sts, 1 tr into next tr (this will now be called "1 open block"), 1 tr into each of next 3 sts (this will now be called "1 solid block"), rep from * to end, working last tr into top of turning ch, turn. 73 blocks.

Row 3: 3 ch (counts as 1 tr), miss tr at end of last row, 2 solid blocks, *1 open block, 1 solid block, rep from * to last block, 1 solid block, working last tr into top of turning ch, turn.

Row 4: 3 ch (counts as 1 tr), miss tr at end of last row, (1 solid block, 1 open block) twice, *1 solid block, 3 open blocks, rep from * to last 5 blocks, (1 solid block, 1 open

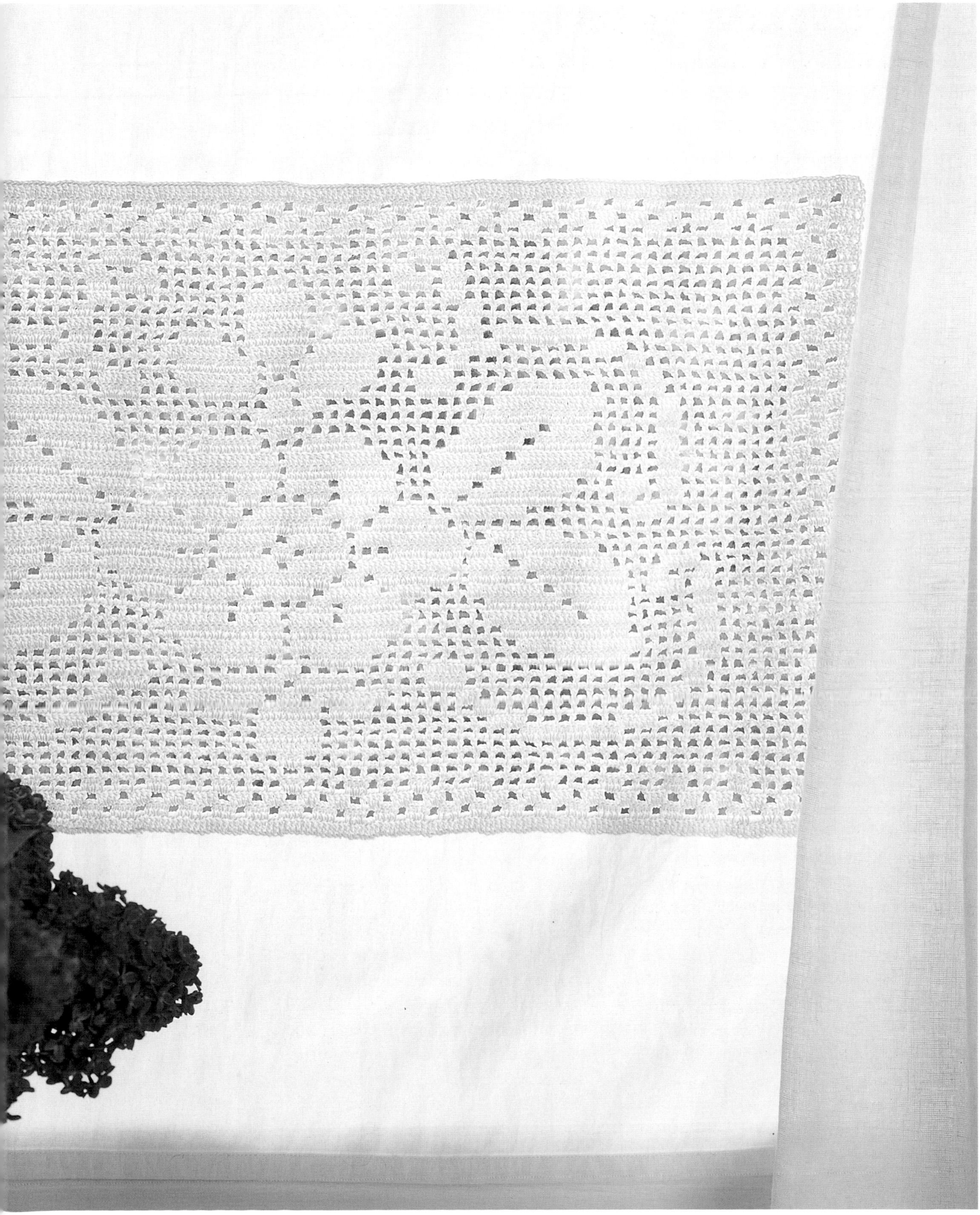

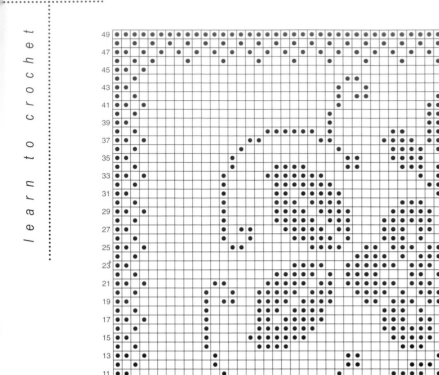

KEY   ☐ = open square   ● = solid block

block) twice, 1 solid block, turn.

Row 5: 3 ch (counts as 1 tr), 2 solid blocks, 1 open block, 1 solid block, 65 open blocks, 1 solid block, 1 open block, 2 solid blocks, turn.

Row 6: 3 ch (counts as 1 tr), 1 solid block, 1 open block, 1 solid block, 33 open blocks, 1 solid block, 33 open blocks, 1 solid block, 1 open block, 1 solid block, turn.

Row 7: 3 ch (counts as 1 tr), 2 solid blocks, 33 open blocks, 3 solid blocks, 33 open blocks, 2 solid blocks, turn.

Row 8: 3 ch (counts as 1 tr), 1 solid block, 1 open block, 1 solid block, 13 open blocks, 6 solid blocks, 13 open blocks, 3 solid blocks, 13 open blocks, 6 solid blocks, 13 open blocks, 1 solid block, 1 open block, 1 solid block, turn.

Row 9: 3 ch (counts as 1 tr), 2 solid blocks, 1 open block, 1 solid block, 10 open blocks, 2 solid blocks, 6 open blocks, 2 solid blocks, 11 open blocks, 3 solid blocks, 11 open blocks, 2 solid blocks, 6 open blocks, 2 solid blocks, 10 open blocks, 1 solid block, 1 open block, 2 solid blocks, turn.

Row 10: 3 ch (counts as 1 tr), 1 solid block, 1 open block, 1 solid block, 10 open blocks, 1 solid block, 10 open blocks, 1 solid block, 7 open blocks, 2 solid blocks, 1 open block, 3 solid blocks, 1 open block, 2 solid blocks, 7 open blocks, 1 solid block, 10 open blocks, 1 solid block, 10 open blocks, 1 solid block, 1 open block, 1 solid block, turn.

These 10 rows set position of design.

Cont as now set, working from chart, until all 49 rows have been completed.

Fasten off.

Pin out to measurement given, cover with a damp cloth and leave to dry naturally.

Once dry, lay crochet panel onto right side of curtain in position required. Stitch in place using a narrow zig-zag stitch worked over the finished edge and through the curtain fabric. Carefully trim away curtain fabric behind crochet panel and oversew the raw edges.

ABOVE: Follow this chart to work the design on the filet panel. Once the first 10 rows have been completed from the written instructions, start by working row 11.

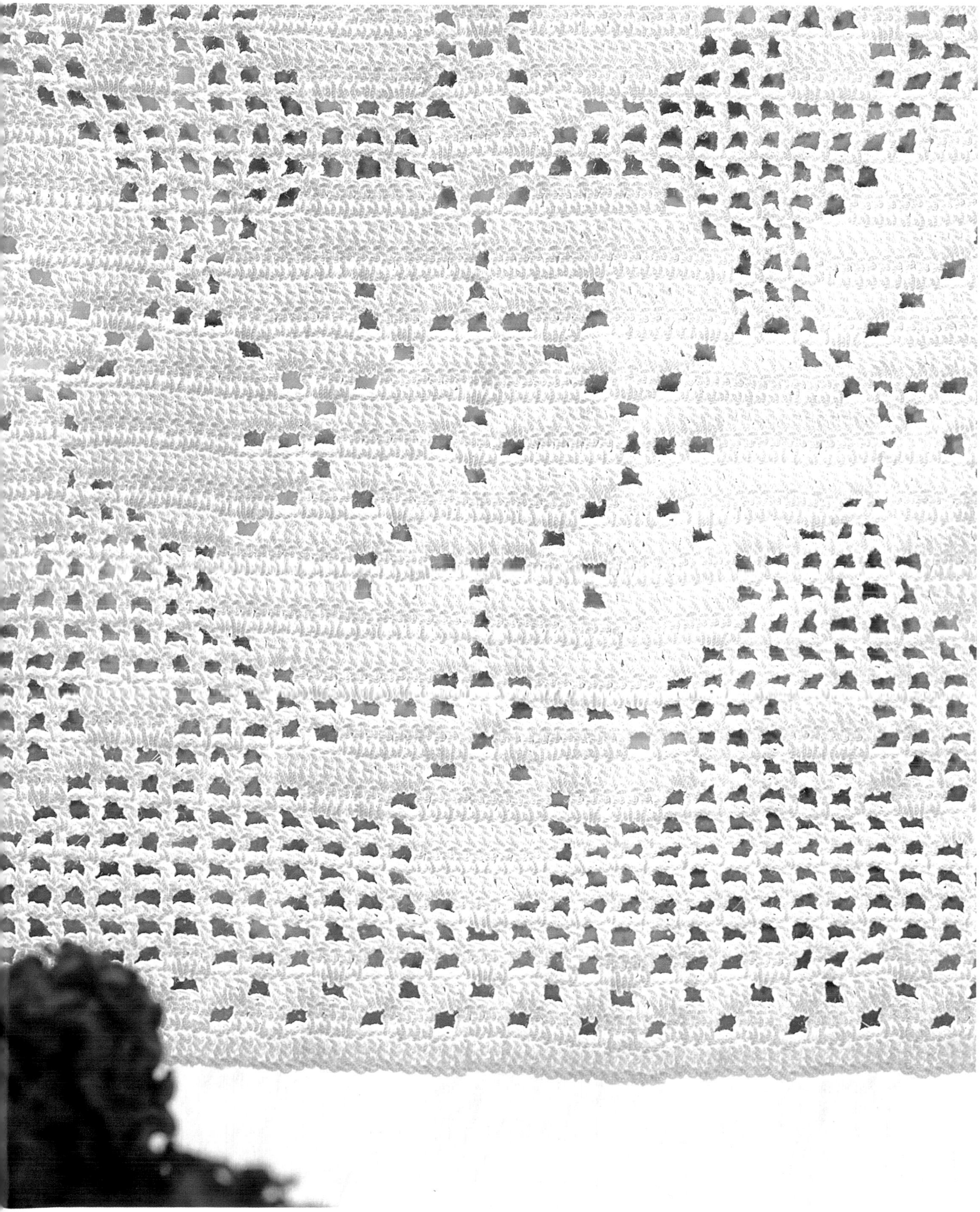

Suppliers

UK

Coats Crafts UK
PO Box 22
Lingfield House
Lingfield Point
McMullen Road
Darlington
Co Durham DL1 1YQ.
Tel: (01325) 394237
E mail: consumer.ccuk@coats.com
Website: www.coatscrafts.co.uk
Suppliers of crochet yarns and hooks,
embroidery and haberdashery supplies.

Jaeger Handknits
Green Lane Mill
Holmfirth
West Yorks HD9 2DX.
Tel: (01484) 680050
Suppliers of hand knitting yarns.

Rowan Yarns
Green Lane Mill
Holmfirth
West Yorks HD9 2DX
Tel: (01484) 681881
E-mail: sales@knitrowan.com
Website: www.knitrowan.com
Suppliers of hand knitting yarns.

Sirdar Spinning Ltd
Flanshaw Lane
Wakefield
West Yorks WF2 9ND
Tel: (01924) 371501.
E-mail: enquiries@sirdar.co.uk
Website: www.sirdar.co.uk
Suppliers of hand knitting yarns.

**Thomas B Ramsden and Co
(Bradford) Ltd**
Netherfield Road
Guiseley
West Yorks LS20 9PD
Tel: (01943) 872264
E-mail: sales@tbramsden.co.uk
Website: www.tbramsden.co.uk
Suppliers of Wendy hand knitting yarns.

SOUTH AFRICA

Arthur Bales
62, 4th Avenue
Linden
Johannesburg 2195
Tel: (011) 888 2401

ABC Knitting & Haberdashery
327 President Street
Germiston 1401
Tel: (011) 873 4296

Trienies
Shop 41, Sanlam Centre
Leraatsfontein
Witbank 1034
Tel: (013) 692 4196

The Image
23 Lynwood Shopping Centre
Lynwood Road
Lynwood Ridge
Pretoria 0081
Tel: (012) 361 1737

Knitting Nook
5 Library Lane
Somerset West
Cape Town 7130
Tel: (021) 852 3044
(Retail and mail order)

Knitting Wool Centre (Pty) Ltd
122 Victoria Road
Woodstock
Cape Town 7925
Tel: (021) 447 1134

Orion Wool Shop and Needlecraft
39 Adderley Street
Cape Town 8000
Tel: (021) 461 6941
Retail and mail order

Little Angel
Shop 4, Newton Spar Centre
3rd Avenue
Newton Park
Port Elizabeth 6045
Tel: (041) 363 9943

Swansdown Knitting Wools (Pty) Ltd
8 Foundry Lane
Durban 4001
Tel: (031) 304 0488

OVS Sewing Machine Centre
Shop 5, The Arcade
Westburger Street
Middestad
Bloemfontein 9301
Tel: (051) 448 9944

AUSTRALIA

Greta's Handcraft Centre
321 Pacific Highway
LINDFIELD
NSW 2070
Tel: (02) 9416 2489

Jo Sharp Pty Ltd
P.O.Box 357
Albany, WA 6331
Tel: (08) 9842 2250
Website: www.josharp.com.au

Knitters of Australia
498 Hampton Street
HAMPTON
VIC 3188
Tel: (03) 9533 1233

Lindcraft
Gallery Level
Imperial Arcade
Pitt Street
SYDNEY
NSW 2000
Tel: (02) 9221 5111

Sunspun
185 Canterbury Rd
CANTERBURY
VIC 3126
Tel: (03) 9830 1609

NEW ZEALAND

Knit World
Selected branches stock Rowan wools,
phone first to find out
Branches nationwide:
Auckland – (09) 837 6111
Tauranga – (07) 577 0797
Hastings – (06) 878 0090
New Plymouth – (06) 758 3171
Palmerston North – (06) 356 8974
Wellington – (04) 385 1918
Christchurch – (03) 379 2300
Dunedin – (03) 477 0400

Spotlight
Branches throughout New Zealand
19 Link Drive
Glenfield
Tel: (09) 444 0220
www.spotlightonline.co.nz

Woolmart Wools
Branches throughout South Island and
Auckland
Check listings in your local White or
Yellow Pages (under "Knitting Wool")

USA

Knitting Fever Inc
35 Debevoise Avenue
Roosevelt
New York 11575, USA
Tel: (516) 546 3600
Website: www.knittingfever.com

CANADA

Diamond Yarns Ltd
155 Martin Ross Avenue
Unit 3, Toronto
Ontario M3J 2L9.
Tel: (416) 736 6111
Website: www.diamondyarn.com

JAPAN

Eisaku Noro & Co Ltd
55 Shimoda Ohibino Azaichou
Ichinomita Aichi, 491 0105
Tel: (81) 52 203 5100

GERMANY

Designer Yarns
Handelsagentur Klaus Koch
Pontinusweg 7, D-50859 Köln,
Tel/Fax: (0234) 77573
Website: www.designer-yarns.de

FRANCE

Elle Tricote
8 Rue de Cog
67000 Strasbourg
Tel: (03) 88 230313
Website: www.elletricote.com.fr

BELGIUM

Pavan
Koningin Astridlaan 78, 9000 Gent
Tel: (9221) 8594
E-mail: pavan@pandora.be

Index

abbreviations 11, 15

Baby Blankets 68–71
Baby Cardigan, Hat and Blanket
    58–65
bags 28–31
bars 73
Bedspread 49–53
blanket, baby 65, 68–71
blocking 48
bobbles 41

cardigan, baby 60–2
centre hole, to close 23
chain space, to work into 66
chain stitch 12
    to work into 13
circular crochet see rounds, working in
cluster 40
colours, to join 26
corners, to edge 47
crab stitch 41
Crochet Bags 28–31
crochet diagram see stitch diagram
cross-body bag 28–31
curtain panel 74–7
curved edge 46–7

darning in ends 10
decreasing 24
double crochet stitch 14
    joining with 25
double treble stitch 14–15
Dressing Table Set 32–5

edging 46–7
    to join 26, 47
    separate 47, 54–7
ends: to darn in 10
    to enclose 26
equipment 8–10

fastening off 15, 23
filet crochet 72–3
Filet Curtain Panel 74–7
flower motif 58–60
foundation chain 12

half treble stitch 14
hat, baby 62–5
Hats 36–9
hook: to hold 12
    to insert 13, 66
    sizes 8, 11

increasing 27

joining: colours 26
    edging 26, 47
    ends of a round 22
    motifs 25
    seams 25
    yarn 26

lacets 73
lacy mats 32–5

mesh see filet crochet
motif: flower 58–60
    to join 25
    lacy 34

needle, sewing 10, 25

pattern repeat 17
pattern, to use 11
picot 40
pins 10
popcorns 41
pressing 10, 25, 48
puffs 41

quadruple treble stitch 15

quintuple treble stitch 15

relief stitches 67
rounds, working in 22–3
row ends, to edge 46
rows, to work 13

Scarves 42–5
scissors 10
seams 10, 25
sextuple treble stitch 15
shaping see decreasing; increasing
shells 40
shopper 28–31
size: of design 11
    of hook 8, 11
slip loop 12
slip stitch 14
stitch diagram 16–17
stitch groups 40–1
stitch repeat 16, 17
stitches: basic 12–15
    to place 13, 66–7
    relief 67
    to work between 67
swatch, tension 11
symbols for stitch diagram 16

tape measure 10
tension 10–11
Throw 18–21
treble stitch 12–13
    relief 67
triple treble stitch 15

turning chain 13, 15

yarn: to hold 12
    to join 26
    quantities 11
    types 9

Acknowledgments

With thanks to the following people for all their help: Mrs Palmer, Julie Gill, Stella Smith, Kathleen Hargreaves, David Rawson, Ola Jankowska and Tricia McKenzie. I would also like to thank Rosemary Wilkinson and Clare Sayer at New Holland, and Shona Wood for her beautiful photographs.